# A
# COMMUNITY
# OF JOY

# EFFECTIVE CHURCH SERIES

## TIM WRIGHT
### Edited by HERB MILLER

# A COMMUNITY OF JOY

## HOW TO CREATE CONTEMPORARY WORSHIP

ABINGDON PRESS
*Nashville*

A COMMUNITY OF JOY:
HOW TO CREATE CONTEMPORARY WORSHIP

**Library of Congress Cataloging-in-Publication Data**

Wright, Tim, 1957–
    A community of joy : how to create contemporary worship/Tim Wright ; edited by Herb Miller.
        p.   cm.—(Effective church series)
    Includes bibliographical references.
    **ISBN 0-687-09117-9** (pbk.:alk. paper)
    1. Public worship.   I. Miller, Herb.   II. Title.   III. Series.
BV15.W75   1994
264—dc20                                                        93-41708

Scripture quotations are from the New Revised Standard Version Bible, Copyright © 1989 by the Division of Christian Education of the National Council of the Churches of Christ in the USA. Used by permission.

Excerpt from *How Can It Be All Right When Everything Is All Wrong?* by Lewis B. Smedes is Copyright © 1982 by Lewis B. Smedes. Reprinted by permission of HarperCollins Publishers, Inc.

Excerpt from *The Best Christmas Pageant Ever* by Barbara Robinson is Copyright © 1972 by Barbara Robinson. Reprinted by permission of HarperCollins Publishers.

94 95 96 97 98 99 00 01 02 03—10 9 8 7 6 5 4 3

MANUFACTURED IN THE UNITED STATES OF AMERICA

*In loving memory of my grandparents,*
*the Reverend W. E. and Ethel Klawitter—*
*their passion for evangelism*
*inspired me to be a pastor*
*"just like Grandpa"*

# CONTENTS

# FOREWORD

"Would you like to have one of our new low-calorie suckers?" a waitress asked one of the "regulars" who drank coffee at the restaurant every morning.

"I suppose," he replied, wondering what was coming. She handed him a sucker stick. The sealed cellophane wrapper that would have covered the candy end was empty.

Some worship services come across that way—like empty wrappers. When that happens consistently, three negatives result: (1) regular worshipers receive insufficient spiritual nurture; (2) new attenders do not return; and (3) other aspects of a congregation's effectiveness suffer. The quality of that 60 minutes—less than one percent of each week—fuels the other 167 hours of the week's ministry. Empty worship empties churches of both people and vitality.

Why, then, do so few church leaders make creative changes? Some stay locked in the status quo because they fear reprisals from tradition-addicted laity. Many leaders, however, keep on manufacturing empty wrappers because they lack how-to resources. Tim Wright addresses this vacuum in a thorough way. His practical ideas fit every type of church, including the mainline liturgical types. An appendix provides leaders with years of worship-service patterns.

This author's leadership insights fit the goal of the Effective Church Series: to help meet the need for how-to answers in specific areas of church life. Each of the volumes in this series provides both clergy and laity with practical insights and methods that can increase a congregation's effectiveness in achieving God's purposes in every aspect of ministry—leadership, worship, Sunday school, membership care, biblical literacy, spiritual growth, small groups, evangelism, new-member assimilation, prayer, youth work, singles ministry, young adult ministry, time management, stewardship, administration, community service, world mission, conflict resolution, and writing skills.

Tim Wright's insights also fit the theological focus of the Effective Church Series. While concentrating more on the practical than on the theoretical and conceptual, this book's "ideas that work" rest on biblical principles. Without that foundation, method-sharing builds on quicksand. Wright has addressed the subject of worship in ways consistent with biblical truths and classic Christian theology.

A computer operator reported difficulty in installing new programs in her machine—until she discovered the cause of the problem. After she cleaned the head of the tape drive—removing dust and lint—the computer could read and save what she was trying to install. Inside every human skull is a computer equipped with RAM (random access memory) and ROM (read only memory). What that fantastic computer can accomplish is determined by (1) the quality of its contents and (2) how it processes the data. Effective worship services do both: They improve the stored information and fine-tune the programming.

What happens if the dust and lint of accumulated tradition reduce worship quality? The people suffer and the church suffers. Worship is a meeting with God. If the worship service content and style prevent people from being fully present at the meeting, wise leaders make adjustments. This author provides interesting, practical suggestions for helping that to happen.

Herb Miller
Lubbock, Texas

# ACKNOWLEDGMENTS

**Thanks—**

To my wife, Jan, for her love and patience: Jan has been my friend, partner, and supporter in ministry. She also serves as the keyboardist for the Good News Band, the group I work with on Sunday mornings. Together, we have dreamed about and implemented visitor-oriented worship. Thanks, too, for putting up with my "quiet" moods as I continually thought about this project.

To my daughter, Alycia, and son, Mike: You two are the best! Thanks for letting me write about you. Most of all, thanks for the privilege of being your dad!

To my mom and dad for bringing me up in the faith: Their encouragement and support over the years helped me believe in myself.

To my brother, Jeff, and his wife, Diane, for working with me in the adventure of visitor-oriented worship. They, along with the Good News Band, have helped me fine-tune many of the principles in this book.

To my father-in-law, Vic Wallestad, who passed away during the writing of this book. He and his wife, Phadoris, who passed away in 1990, supported my family during my seminary years. They also planted the seed that brought me to Community Church of Joy. Their impact on my life and ministry has been significant. I Thank God for them.

## ACKNOWLEDGMENTS

To Pastor Walt Kallestad, my friend and senior pastor: He continually affirms me and gives me the freedom to experiment. None of this would have been possible without his encouragement. It takes a special person of God to allow an associate so much freedom.

To all the pastors, staff, and family of Joy: They have made the call of pastoring an absolute delight.

To Herb Miller and the people at Abingdon Press for their encouragement.

To all who have contributed to this project: Your insights and stories will encourage others to dream new dreams.

To Jesus Christ, who made me his through the waters of baptism and has never let go. To him be the glory!

"Go therefore and make disciples of all nations,
baptizing them in the name of the Father
and of the Son and of the Holy Spirit,
and teaching them to obey everything
that I have commanded you."

Matthew 28:19-20

# I

# "WE'VE NEVER DONE IT THAT WAY BEFORE!"

Sunday, 11:20 A.M.: 550 people begin to gather inside the worship center. The buzz of anticipation fills the sanctuary as they greet one another and find their seats. Taped music plays in the background.

At 11:30, the music fades. Three vocalists, backed by piano, bass guitar, rhythm guitar, lead guitar, and drums, take the stage. Their call to worship sounds similar to the music heard on pop radio stations. The audience settles in and begins to clap along.

After the group sings, the pastor welcomes the people and gives them the opportunity to shake hands with those around them and introduce themselves. After relating a personal anecdote, he directs the worshipers' attention to a large screen up front. Words to a contemporary worship chorus flash upon it. The band teaches the song to the congregation, which quickly joins in. The service continues with more music from the band, a Bible reading, and a drama. It concludes with a message by the pastor on the subject of stress.

Can this be worship?

## *The Changing Face of Worship*

Around the United States and throughout the world, something radically new is happening—something that has been taking shape over the last twenty years. From Phoenix, Arizona, to Seattle, Washington; from Calgary in Alberta, Canada, to Endicott, New York; from Nuriootpa, Australia, to Minneapolis, Minnesota; the face of worship is changing. Across denominational lines, congregations are creating, developing, and experimenting with innovative styles of worship and music.

Two factors fuel this new climate of innovation: (1) Today's new "customer"; and (2) a growing sense of mission on the part of congregations.

## *No Longer Business as Usual*

The generations born after 1946 have forever changed the way people choose churches. The values, motivations, and ambitions of these young to middle-age adults differ from those of previous generations. What worked in the past will not work today. Churches can no longer do business as usual.

In the past, most people chose a church for one or more of three reasons:

### Denominational Affiliation

Presbyterians joined Presbyterian churches; Methodists worshiped with the Methodists; Episcopalians attended Episcopal churches. The Lutheran Church, like all others, structured itself around this loyalty factor. The denominational hymnal enabled Lutherans to worship comfortably anywhere in the country. Lutherans assumed that Lutherans wanted to worship like Lutherans, with other Lutherans.

### Church Doctrine

A few people crossed denominational lines, but usually only if the doctrine was close to what they believed.

## Location

Before the days of freeways and long commutes, churchgoers valued close proximity. Congregations, responding to this need, promoted themselves as neighborhood churches. They appealed to and served those living within their shadows.

Though influential in years past, those three reasons no longer motivate today's customers. For the new generation of church shoppers, denominational loyalty is out, and denominational and church doctrine no longer play a prominant role in influencing their choice. Nearby location is far less important now than in former days.

## Consumer-oriented Church Shoppers

People now choose churches in much the same way they make all other choices—as consumers (not necessarily as believers). They go where the action is—where they think their needs will be met—regardless of denomination, apparent doctrine, or location.

For consumers, the worship service is one of the major reasons for choosing a church. Because they value worship style, most shoppers visit several churches before making their decision. On each visit, before the service is over, most of them will have decided whether they intend to come back. In other words, we have no second chance to make a good first impression. If the service is dull and irrelevant, people will continue their search. If the service is alive and practical, their shopping has ended (for the time being, anyway).

For congregations committed to reaching new people, the implications warrant serious consideration: Attracting and reaching the unchurched means a thorough and sympathetic understanding of their unique values and motivations. It means seeing life and church through their eyes. It means designing worship services that correspond to their needs and values.

## Why Believers Worship

Christians gather for worship each week for many different reasons, among which the following are most important.

17

**We worship to worship.** We gather together to praise and thank God. As a child, I once told my mom that church was boring, that I did not get anything out of it. She replied, "We don't go to church to get. We go to give. We go to give praise to God." She is absolutely correct. Believers gather to give praise to the One who loves us. We meet each week to thank and adore the One who gave his best for us. We worship God because God is indeed worthy of our praise. Worship is the joy-filled response of those whose lives have been transformed by Jesus Christ.

**We worship to pass on the tradition of faith.** As believers gather, they pass on the faith from generation to generation. As a child sitting in the pew of our little church, the faith was instilled in me. God nurtured my faith through the liturgy and the messages. The same happens to my children as they attend worship. Millions of others around the world experience that encounter with faith each Sunday. Through worship, we pass the candle of faith.

**We worship to experience friendship.** In worship, we gather with other believers and encourage one another. Meeting friends, praying together, crying and laughing together—this makes worship human and tangible. It puts flesh on the gospel.

These three values drive and shape worship services the world over. As valid and solid as they are, however, these priorities have one major problem: They center solely on the needs of those already in the faith. Setting the worship agenda by focusing on the needs of believers excludes many of the unchurched guests.

## Consumerism Comes to the Church

When nonchurched people or marginal members from another church visit a congregation, they bring an entirely different agenda. As consumers, their expectations differ dramatically from those of believers. When irreligious people visit a congregation, they come asking, "What's in it for me? How will this worship service make me feel? Will it help me meet my goals in life? Does it have anything relevant to say to me?"

Consumers come to worship with a unique set of values that is often at odds with the teachings of the church. By recognizing and responding to these values, however, congregations will more effectively reach new people. Consumers value:

## 1. Innovation

Consumers value the new, the up-to-date, and the trendy. Raised in a period of unprecedented technological change, they value fast action and creative applications. Yet, many of the churches they visit use worship services based on a sixteenth-century model. Today's consumers still desire the structure, stability, and sameness that worship offers. But without innovations and "surprises," the service quickly becomes boring and lifeless.

## 2. Instant Gratification

Consumers want worship services to offer them something practical, something they can use every day. They want a gospel that applies to all of life: family, career, health, finances, time, and so on. However, many leave worship frustrated because they miss the connection between the gospel and their world.

## 3. Choices

Forty percent of all TV viewers first flip through most of the channels, and then choose![1] Consumers do the same with churches. They look for the best option. Today's generations were raised with a shopping-mall mentality. They value a variety of choices under one roof. In visiting some congregations, however, they find very few options. For example, many churches offer only one style of worship.

Likewise, denominational churches use the same style of worship from congregation to congregation throughout the entire country. The message to guests comes through loud and clear: "This is the way we worship. You can conform to our way or go somewhere else." And many shoppers do just that.

They gravitate to the churches that offer different choices of worship styles.

## 4. Quality
Consumers demand excellence. They will not settle for mediocrity in the church. Quality-conscious congregations attract quality-conscious consumers.

## 5. Short-term Commitments
Because life is so hectic, people make fewer and fewer long-term commitments. Yet, congregations tend to weave long-term commitments into their overall structure, effectively keeping new people out. Two-year Bible studies and months-long volunteer assignments discourage people from involvement.

## 6. The Present
Having grown up in a fragile world, people born after 1946 value a present-day orientation. Their agenda focuses on today, not tomorrow or yesterday. When visiting church on Sunday, however, they often hear music from previous generations. They see religious garb and symbols from centuries past. They experience worship services based on models from former times—models that now seem irrelevant and unintelligible.

## 7. Intimacy
Intimacy is becoming a lost art in our country, creating an almost insatiable appetite for relationships. We live in a day of disenfranchised people. The traditional family of the 1950s and 1960s has all but disappeared, and families continue to break down. Video games and TVs baby-sit latchkey kids while mom and dad work. People relate more to cash machines and computers than to other people. As John Naisbitt reminds us in *Megatrends*, a high-tech society demands high touch. People today crave intimacy. They want to be known and loved for who they are. They come to church in the hope that someone will love them, that someone will accept them just as they are. They value a warm, open environment. Worship services that

promote intimacy and relationships will win them over. Stuffy, unfriendly congregations will repel them.

## 8. Experiences

Persons born after 1946 are highly experience-oriented. Their hunger for experiences has taken them down some unique paths: drugs, the Jesus People Movement, EST, the New Age movement, sex. As they age, these people continue to value and desire experiences. New sources for today's experience-seeking generations include leisure and learning.

Part of their need for experience grows out of the perceived failure and sterility of science. The post-World War II generation grew up in a technologically based world. Science and technology were believed to be the answer to all of life's problems. Through them, all disease would be cured. All wars would cease. Poverty would be eliminated. However, none of these hopes were realized. Disease did not end. The poverty rate continues to climb. Rather than building a better world, technology was viewed as the culprit behind the Bomb and Vietnam. Science did not hold the key to a better life after all. It failed to keep its promises.

In addition to letting people down, technology also robbed them of joy. Life became too rational. It was programmed to the point of boredom. So, hoping to stimulate their neglected emotions and spirituality, many post-1946 babies turned their attention to experiences.

Another factor behind this need for experience is the personality of the post-World War II generation. Where previous generations were outward-driven, today's generations are more motivated by internal satisfactions. Past generations banded together to fight World Wars, build monuments, and plan highway infrastructures. Outward accomplishments provided their motivation. Those born after 1946 value inner motivation over outward accomplishments. Rather than build, they philosophize and justify.

This need for experience affects their view of the church. Irreligious people visit churches in the hope of encountering God personally. They not only want to know *about* God; they want to *know* God. They desire a living, dynamic faith, a faith

21

that stimulates them intellectually and emotionally. Styles of worship tell them everything about the kind of experience they can expect in a congregation. Dull, lifeless worship equals a dull, lifeless God. Vibrant, dynamic worship says that God is alive and can be experienced.

### 9. Contemporary Expressions

During the 1960s and 1970s, young people rebelled against anything and everything traditional. Refusing to trust anyone over age thirty, they rejected the values of the past. They replaced Christianity with Eastern religions and the New Age movement. They exchanged democracy for socialist ideas. They opted to live together outside of marriage. They reshaped childbearing with the advent of the pill and other new forms of birth control. They traded in suits and ties for long hair and ragged jeans. They turned their backs on classical music and replaced it with a brand new sound: rock and roll.

Rock and roll rallied young people during that era. It fueled their rebellion. It not only reflected their values; it shaped them. Rock offered young people a common voice. It spoke their language and gave vent to their concerns. Contemporary music was *the* uniting force behind this unique generation.

Today, nontraditional life-styles continue to impact culture and ministry. So does this nontraditional music. Rock and roll, in some form or another, is here to stay. Contemporary music—pop, rock, country/western, rap—continues to be the heart music of today's generations. As people shop for a church, they look for congregations that value them by valuing their music. In designing worship services attractive to today's consumers, no factor has greater impact than the choice of music.

### 10. Pragmatism

Church shoppers today are extremely pragmatic. They want to see exactly how the scientific advances will be applied technologically to each of them. Their need for the practical led to the mushrooming of "self-help" and "how-to" books in the 1970s and 1980s. In choosing a church, these pragmatists value messages that offer them practical help for daily living. They want to know not only that Jesus loves them but how to apply that love in their lives. Lectures on the latest theological trends will not impress them. They want practical messages that can change their lives.

### 11. Authenticity
People crave heroes. They want someone who will be honest, someone who can be counted on, someone willing to be vulnerable. Visitors hope to find such authenticity in the church. If the congregation is unfriendly, guests will conclude that authenticity is not a high priority. Worship services couched in overly religious jargon—with staid, lifeless sermons—will add to that perception. The worship guests' perception may or may not be true, but for them, perception is reality.

Churches can create a climate of integrity and authenticity through warm, inviting, less formal services. Couple that climate with honest, down-to-earth messages, and the worship experience becomes a magnet, drawing in the unchurched.

## Responding to Consumer Values

Not all the values that guests bring to worship are compatible with Christianity; nor are such values confined solely to the irreligious. Believers also embrace some of these same values as they shop for a church home. However, in order to effectively reach new people, congregations must find ways to attract their attention. By creatively responding to consumer values, without compromising integrity, churches can impact people with the gospel.

## A New Passion for Mission

New consumer values are changing the face of worship. But worship is undergoing a transformation for another important reason: mission. After decades of declining church membership, mainline congregations and denominations are looking for new ways to impact secular society. Innovative worship, focused on the unchurched, grows out of this desire.

Congregations all across the United States are beginning to re-embrace the Great Commission. Rather than seeing the Sunday-morning service strictly from a worship perspective, they view it from a mission orientation. In designing services, worship leaders now ask, "How can we use worship to attract and hold irreligious people?"

They see the discouraged, alienated people of their community. They see the emptiness and brokenness. They see the lostness. And they want to reach out. They no longer say, "We have never done it that way before!" Instead, congregations are dreaming new dreams. They are taking risks in designing new, creative styles of worship. These innovations are not fueled by the need to be a part of the latest fad or trend. Rather, a God-given passion to reach lost people motivates the change. The desire to be in touch with God's heart, to see God's kingdom grow, shapes the worship experience.

A pastor was touring a children's unit of a large Southern California hospital. Walking down the hallway, he could hear the cries of babies ringing off the walls. He followed a nurse into one of the rooms, where he noticed a child about one year old lying in a crib. The baby was covered with horrible bruises, scratches, and scars. The pastor at first thought the child had been in a severe accident. On closer examination, however, he was shocked to see obscenities written in ink all over the child's legs. The baby had been abused. Because of internal injuries, the baby was unable to hold down food. The bottom of his feet were scarred with cigarette burns.

The pastor watched as the nurse reached down to pick up the baby. Tenderly and gently, she lifted the child, holding him next to her. The child began to scream, suspect of any kind of human touch. But as she held the baby securely, he slowly began to quiet. Finally, in spite of the wounds, hurts, and past experiences, love broke through to the baby's heart. Because of that love, he no longer felt the need to cry.

Hurting people, people bruised and battered by life, surround our churches. They need hope. They need healing. They need someone willing to risk reaching out to them with the love of Christ. Mission—the passion to reach them—is changing the face of worship around the world.

## *Crucial Questions*

The Spirit is indeed doing a new thing in the area of worship and mission. But this new work raises several questions, and congregations seeking to impact a secular society will take these questions seriously:

What keeps people from coming to church? What can we do to encourage them to come? What are their values? How can we, with integrity, design worship experiences that take these values seriously?

For liturgically oriented congregations, the question might be: Can liturgical worship impact an unchurched society?

ROSE CITY PARK
UNITED METHODIST CHURCH
5830 NE Alameda
Portland, OR. 97213
503-281-1229

*"And if the bugle gives an indistinct sound,
who will get ready for battle?
So with yourselves;
if in a tongue you utter speech that is not intelligible,
how will anyone know what is being said?
For you will be speaking into the air."*
I Corinthians 14:8-9

## II

# LITURGICAL WORSHIP AND THE UNCHURCHED

Until I started fourth grade, my family attended a small Lutheran church in St. Louis Park, Minnesota. I sat in the front row faithfully every Sunday. I had to. My mom played the organ, and the organ stood in the front of the church.

At the time, Lutherans worshiped from the *Service Book and Hymnal,* warmly referred to as the "Red Hymnal." One Sunday after church, I remember saying to my mom that I did not understand the service. The language and music seemed so bizarre and difficult. Instead of taking offense, she responded in a way that helped me see liturgy in a different light. She pointed out the biblical foundation of liturgical worship, that Bible verses filled the liturgy. She told me that as I learned the liturgy, I committed those verses to memory; the Word of God was being seared into my heart week after week.

Mom's insights gave me a new appreciation for the "Red Hymnal" and liturgical worship. Years later, I can still sing from memory bits and pieces of the service.

## *The Pluses of Liturgical Worship*

Liturgical worship has a rich, deep heritage in many established denominations. For believers in Jesus Christ it holds several important values:

First of all, liturgical worship is *Bible-based.* Most liturgical services come directly from the pages of Scripture.

Second, liturgical worship is *worship-facilitating.* Drawing us into the action, it moves us from passive spectators to active participants.

Third, liturgical worship is *God-centered.* It gives us a sense of the majesty of God. It inspires us with awe. It reminds us that God is over all, supporting the universe. Liturgical worship moves us with the power and wonder of God.

Believers all over the world find themselves deeply impacted by liturgical worship each Sunday. It remains a valid, inspiring, biblical form of worship.

## *Drawbacks to Liturgical Worship*

Liturgical worship as seen through the eyes of a first-time visitor, however, reveals some drawbacks. Liturgical worship actually erects several barriers or obstacles to reaching non-churched people, people who are totally unfamiliar with any style of worship.

**Barrier 1—Liturgical worship confuses people.** The latest Lutheran Book of Worship, or "Green Hymnal," has two main sections: The liturgy, found by using page numbers; and the section of hymns, which starts the page-numbering process all over again. Therein lies the beginning of confusion in Lutheran services (and similar complications can be found in other mainline services).

When worship leaders direct people to page 76 in the hymnal, visitors flip over to hymn 76. By the time they realize their mistake and turn to *page* 76, the rest of the congregation has moved on to *hymn* 76. The congregation stands while the guests continue to fumble along. By the time they stand, the congregation sits. The result: abject frustration.

One pastor tells of attending a liturgical worship service several years ago. He happened to sit near some visitors who looked completely lost during the liturgy, and he tried to help them find their way through the hymnal. But after several minutes of confusion and frustration, they slammed the book in disgust. They surrendered and gave up. It happens more than we realize. And the odds are that they will never come back.

Bob Orr, from Church Growth, Inc., shared the following statistics in a worship seminar: In 1952, 6 percent of our population was not religiously trained. (Stated positively, this means that in that year, 94 percent of our population was religiously trained.) By 1988, however, 35 percent of our population was *not* religiously trained.[1] Some suggest that of those age 35 and under, 70 to 75 percent have *not* been religiously trained. Liturgical worship confuses new people because it assumes religious training. It assumes that the worshipers have been members from the cradle, or at least understand the experience. But fewer and fewer people do.

When I entered the fourth grade, my family left the Lutheran church and joined an Evangelical Free church. That change began a journey through several different denominations. I attended a Covenant high school. I married a Presbyterian and worshiped at her church for a couple of years. I spent one year at a Baptist seminary. However, I knew I would eventually return to the Lutheran church. My heart and mind respond best to Lutheran theology.

When I finally came back, I discovered that the hymnals had changed. The "Red Hymnal" had been replaced by a "Green Hymnal." I still knew how to follow the liturgy. Yet it took me four Sundays to understand the new book. Imagine the struggle of those totally uninitiated to such a form of worship! They often do not have the required perseverance. One lay member of a worship committee put it this way:

> People would like to have someone talk to them about the Bible, explain the confusing things about religion, and help them understand what it's about.
> Jesus spent His life teaching people they are a family, and if

31

they want to be close to God, they must find Him in one another, not in ritual. . . .

Liturgy was designed by theologians, and it is complicated for ordinary people. People have problems, they hurt, they need comfort and support. To come to church and watch a cold formal service and hear a sermon they can't understand, leaves them cold and undernourished. They walk out of church still hungry.

**Barrier 2—Liturgical worship uses religious language.** One would expect religious language in a religious service. But liturgical worship uses language that the average person on the street cannot comprehend, and I suspect the same can be said for many "churched" people.

Again, liturgical worship assumes religious training. Words, phrases, and titles, such as *litany, absolution, Lent;* the *Nicene, Apostles,* and *Athanasian creeds;* and even *Gospel,* have no meaning for the unchurched. And what people perceive as meaningless and irrelevant, they quickly tune out.

**Barrier 3—Liturgical worship seems unrelated to life.** Because the spiritual often fails to connect with real life in liturgical worship, visitors leave unimpressed. They see pastors wearing long white or black robes. If the pastor happens to be male, they wonder why he is wearing a dress. No one wears clothes like that in the real world (except in airports to raise money).

An "other-worldly" atmosphere permeates the sanctuary and worship experience. Newcomers observe unintelligible symbols and gestures which hold no meaning for them. Those around them apparently understand the symbols, but no one offers visitors an explanation. This shuts guests out of the worship experience, conveying the message that only the liturgically initiated belong in the service.

**Barrier 4—Liturgical worship tends to be unsingable.** Few experiences can move people as much as well-done liturgical music. The music soars stylistically, lyrically, and theologically. Unfortunately, most of it is written by professionally trained, classically oriented musicians, and thus targets only professionally trained, classically oriented members.

The style and difficulty of liturgical music assumes that most people in the pews have musical training. However, children no longer receive the kind of musical training offered years ago. In order to tighten their shrinking budgets, many schools find it necessary to drop their music programs. Such training continues to decrease, along with religious training, making liturgical worship inaccessible to the masses.

Technology further fuels the problem. Today's world of Walkmans and portable CD players has shaped a generation of listeners—not singers.

This holds particularly true for men. Over the years, Christianity has had a hard time winning men. Part of that difficulty originates in the structure of worship services. When it comes to reaching men, liturgical worship has three strikes against it:

Men, generally speaking, do not like to sing, and liturgical services utilize a lot of singing (strike 1).

Bob Orr says that through the years, the typical male voice has lowered by two steps.[2] For many men today, liturgical worship is pitched too high (strike 2).

Add to these the difficulty in singing most liturgical music (strike 3), and men stay away from worship.

**Barrier 5—Liturgical worship uses classically oriented music.** Most people in liturgical churches appreciate classical music. However, classical music accounts for only 2 percent of all music sold in the United States. A very small segment of the population listens to it. Relatively few cities can support a classical station, because of low listenership.

The generations born after 1946 have forever changed the course of music. By far, their number-one music preference is adult contemporary—the heart language of today's generations. They will not develop a craving for classical music as they age, nor will they mature into it. They will rock and roll to their graves.

Yet, most established churches put all their emphasis on the classical style, targeting the 2 percent of the population who enjoy that kind of music. Unfortunately, many in liturgical churches assume that everyone appreciates the same kind of music they do. Research, record sales, and radio stations tell a different story. Reaching new generations of people means finding new forms of worship and music. Fortunately, God is still in the business of inspiring composers, even pop and rock composers.

**Barrier 6—Liturgical worship lacks intimacy.** By its very nature, liturgical worship inspires awe. It focuses on the majesty and power of God. It emphasizes a vertical relationship with God, rather than a horizontal relationship with others.

Liturgical worship may actually work against intimacy: Silence and contemplation reign before the service, rather than conversation. Liturgically designed sanctuaries, built with high, arching ceilings, seem cold and impersonal. Seating arrangements keep people from seeing the faces of other worshipers. The rows of pews force people to focus on the backs of heads and the altar area. Liturgical worship generates little in the way of intimacy and warmth.

Liturgical worship will always be a vital, important option. It will continue to hold meaning for many people. However, the format and music of liturgical worship erects barriers against reaching new people—barriers that turn them off.

With some fine-tuning, congregations can help newcomers overcome those obstacles. Without compromising the integrity of the service, leaders can remove many barriers by warming up the liturgy, and by committing passionately to retrain those who choose to participate.

*The church is the only society in the world*
*that exists for its non-members.*
Archbishop Temple

# III

# MAKING LITURGICAL WORSHIP VISITOR-FRIENDLY

A Lincoln, Nebraska, pastor encourages congregations to "put on the shoes of a first-time visitor to your church":

> If you are using words like Introit . . . Kyrie . . . Collect, and so on, do you explain them or replace them with more understandable directions? How understandable is the "sacramental" portion of your service to new people? How comfortable is the pace of your worship? Do you give verbal direction during the service, or is it assumed that because it's in the bulletin, people should know what comes next in the service? What if Mom has a kid under each arm and can't get to the bulletin? How much sitting or standing do you do in your services? I once heard a man who had been standing too long say, "O.K., pastor, you win, you can stand longer than I can!" He sat down halfway through verse 12 of an opening hymn!

Liturgical worship, by its very nature, is driven by formality. Being God-directed rather than people-directed, it lacks the relational and intimacy aspects of worship that people value today. "Warming up" a liturgical service, adding relational aspects, will help overcome that lack of intimacy. It also

37

compensates for the other barriers inherent in liturgical worship.

## *Warming Up Liturgical Worship*

**1. Begin the morning with prayer.** Mass chaos often rules before the service starts. Pastors, worship leaders, and ushers find themselves rushing around, trying to shore up last-minute details. By the time the service begins they feel frazzled and start the service emotionally and spiritually unprepared.

Several years ago, Community Church of Joy in Phoenix, Arizona, developed a prayer team. This team comes to church an hour early, to pray for the pastors and the worship services. They spend the first half hour praying together as a group. When the pastors arrive, the people in the team gather around them, lay hands on them, and pray for them. After twenty minutes of prayer, they celebrate Communion. Then the worship leaders still have fifteen minutes to attend to any last-minute details and greet people before the service begins.

Starting the day with prayer proves invaluable. It helps us to settle down and focus on our purpose. It puts things in perspective. Prayer reminds us that we serve in God's power, not our own. A dynamic sense of confidence comes when we commit the service to God through prayer.

In starting a prayer team, pray and look for a small group of prayer-minded people. Every congregation has people who would feel honored to pray for the pastors and worship leaders. Once recruited, invite them to meet with the worship team for prayer before the service starts.

Some lay people may feel uncomfortable in laying hands on their pastors and praying for them. Joining hands in a "prayer circle" may prove less threatening and will encourage greater participation. The laying on of hands can be used once people get to know one another.

Prayer makes a positive difference in the attitudes of those leading worship. It also brings about a greater response from the worshipers.

**2. Develop a strong corps of greeters and ushers.** No group of people contributes more to the effectiveness of a service than the ushers and greeters. They set the "climate" as people drive onto the church campus and enter the sanctuary. Friendly greeters create a warm, welcoming environment. Grumpy, gruff, or apathetic ushers turn people off.

People crave a warm, caring touch. In our high-tech society, we value people who greet us with a warm smile, a hug, or a handshake. We find ourselves attracted to people who treat us well, enhance our sense of worth, and help us feel accepted. Such love and care help people open up to the gospel.

Several years ago, our congregation implemented a new worship schedule. This new schedule enabled me to drive to church with my family for the first time in my ministry.

My wife was thrilled. Almost too thrilled, I thought. I used to sit on the platform Sunday mornings and watch as she walked into church. I never understood why she looked so disheveled. Her hair shot out in weird configurations, and she often wore a look of exasperation. I quickly discovered the reason on that first Sunday when we went to church as a family.

I told my kids on Saturday night that we had to leave the house no later than 9:30 on Sunday morning. No problem. They assured me they would be ready. I had a nice, leisurely Sunday morning, got dressed, and by 9:30, I was ready to go. I called for the kids. My daughter responded with a screech. She still had to do her hair. My son could not find his shoes. The longer I waited, the more upset I became. I started to yell. My kids started to yell. Even my wife was yelling. I could feel my hair starting to shoot out in strange angles. I sensed a look of exasperation growing on my face.

Finally, in anger, I jumped into my car and took off. Right behind me in the van was my wife, with our two kids. In my rearview mirror, I could see that she was still yelling at them. We all arrived at church frustrated, upset, and angry. Our spirits were closed. And I was supposed to lovingly preach the gospel!

Many people come to church in similar shape. If not from a fight with the kids, then from the heartache of an illness. If not from a bad week at the office, then from a broken marriage at home. People bring all kinds of hurts and struggles with them into church. A warm, friendly smile can help them open up, settle down, and prepare for the worship experience.

Ushers serve primarily to love and care for people. Certainly, they need to pass out bulletins, take up the collection, and help seat people. But their number-one function is to meet the needs of guests: Make sure visitors find their way around; help them feel at home; answer their questions.

Greeters serve the same function. They too love and care for people. The more of them positioned around the church campus, the warmer the church will seem. Greeters standing near the parking lot offer guests an immediate welcome. As people arrive, greeters can direct them to Sunday-school rooms, the nursery, or the sanctuary. Placing greeters by the doors of the sanctuary provides another opportunity to welcome people.

Recruiting a few "rovers," people trained to spot those standing alone, also makes the campus friendlier. While "official greeters" wear name tags, "rovers" wear no form of identification. They serve as "official, unofficial" greeters—regular members offering friendship to those who need it. People expect "official greeters" to welcome them. A greeting from a "regular, everyday church member," however, impresses newcomers. The ideal plan: Train all members to be "rovers"!

Parking-lot attendants also play a vital role on the welcoming team. Even if the church has adequate parking space, attendants can be utilized. More than traffic managers, these people function as the first line of hosts and hostesses. They offer a warm, friendly smile as people drive onto the church campus. They answer questions. They point people in the right direction. The primary task of parking lot attendants is not to park cars, but to welcome guests.

Providing coffee, doughnuts, fruit, and punch between services also highlights the friendliness of the congregation. People tend to relax and open up around food. Refreshments give them the opportunity to hang around and mingle. Hosts and hostesses, trained to serve people, further promote the welcoming atmosphere of the congregation.

Loving, caring ushers, greeters, hosts, hostesses, and parking-lot attendants help set a warm, positive climate for the worship service.

**3. Make the campus visitor-friendly.** When people visit a church, they come with many anxieties: fear of walking in late; concern about how to find the nursery; nervousness over which door to use when entering the sanctuary, just to name a few. They want to find their way around the church easily and conveniently without looking foolish.

Unfortunately, most congregations assume that everyone knows where everything is. The lack of signs proves it. Posting signs and directions quickly warms up a church campus. Signs tell people that the congregation wants them to find their way around. Signs help visitors feel comfortable and at home.

A highly visible welcome booth provides another effective tool for making the campus visitor-friendly. Staffed with informed people, welcome booths serve several functions. They offer a centralized point where guests can seek out help. They serve as a place where people can register for classes or special events. They contain information packets offering an overview of the church. Welcome booths allow congregations to better service the needs of their visitors and members.

Visitor-friendly churches continually ask the following questions:

Does the church have plenty of visible, attractive signs?

Can visitors find their way around the campus if no one can be found to guide them?

Can they find the office, nursery, or restroom by simply following the signs?

Can they easily find the main entrance to the sanctuary?

**4. Start right.** Rick Muchow, Music Pastor of Saddleback Valley Community Church in Mission Viejo, California, advises:

> It is a mistake to assume that people are ready and prepared to worship when they first arrive on Sunday morning. Usually, they need to "wake up" first. We believe you wake up the Body by waking up the bodies! So we intentionally choose a song with a strong, fast beat and a bright melody that people can move to.

41

The way a service begins sets the tone for the entire worship experience. Starting with a spirit of expectation and excitement prepares people for the gospel. It readies them to receive all God has for them. Today's consumers seek out worship services that say from the start: "God is present, and something dynamic is about to happen!"

Some congregations begin the worship service with a time of confession and forgiveness. Long time churchgoers may appreciate opening with this important liturgical rite, but starting the service with confession and forgiveness says to guests: "You are sinners!" For years, some people stayed away from church, fearing such condemnation. Finally, having the courage to come, they hear from the start how bad they are—that they cannot worship until they confess their failures and shortcomings.

The assurance of forgiveness undoubtedly sets the climate for a dynamic experience. It provides the basis and motivation for worship. However, guests, particularly the unchurched, tend to get stuck on the apparent condemnation and miss the forgiveness. As will be discussed at greater length in chapter VI, people today do not see their problem as sin. They only see their hurts and struggles. As believers, we understand that sin may be at the root of those hurts and struggles. But before guests can hear about confession and forgiveness, their hurts must be addressed. Confession and forgiveness, though a vital part of the service, does not create an inviting beginning for visitors. This in no way suggests that confession and forgiveness should be dropped from the service. Moving it to a later point in the service will help guests settle in and prepare for it. Emphasizing forgiveness as the motivation for confession will make the experience more meaningful for them.

Opening the service with a dynamic choir anthem creates a climate of expectancy. Singing a strong, powerful, inspiring hymn sets an atmosphere of praise. Setting a climate from the beginning that says, "Something dramatic is going to happen!" tunes people into the action. People value experience-oriented services. They want to know that God is present. They come to celebrate. Starting right sets that climate of celebration.

Allowing people to greet one another near the beginning of the service adds further warmth to worship. An encouraging handshake or a "Good morning" builds the sense of intimacy that people desire. Some congregations use the liturgical tradition of "passing the peace" as a form of greeting. Believers shake hands with one another and say, "The peace of the Lord be with you," or something similar. But unchurched people find "passing the peace" uncomfortable. They have no idea what it means or even how to "pass" it. "Passing the peace," while potentially relational, is an unintelligible religious rite for most unchurched people. It often serves only to confuse and embarrass visitors.

People, both churched and unchurched, pass the peace every day by saying, "Good morning!" Encouraging that kind of greeting puts guests at ease. If using the rite of "passing the peace," take the time to explain it and how to pass it. Guests will feel less intimidated.

**5. Use name tags.** An Iowa pastor says, "Identify visitors without drawing attention to them. Avoid procedures that translate into: 'Will all our visitors please stand and turn bright red?'"

Guests want to be noticed, but they do not want to stand out. They want someone to acknowledge their presence without making a scene. They do not want to stand and introduce themselves. (The number-one fear of most people is public speaking.) Nor do they want someone else to introduce them.

Name tags provide an easy, nonthreatening way to recognize guests without embarrassing them. The key to name-tag effectiveness: Invite members and visitors alike to wear similar name tags. Unfortunately, churches often fail to see the value in that procedure—so they distribute name tags only to the visitors.

After visiting a church that gave name tags to visitors only, my daughter, Alycia, said, "It sure was nice to be given name tags. But I wish the people in the church would have worn name tags, too. They knew who I was, but I didn't know them." If given the opportunity, most worship guests would say something similar. Giving name tags only to visitors says to them, "I want to know you, but there is no way you are going to get to know me!"

Providing sticky-backed name tags for all worshipers can help create a friendly climate. They enable people to put a name with a face. Many churches put several of these tags in a welcome folder, a nice looking folder with pockets on the inside.

In those churches, the ushers distribute a welcome folder to each row at the beginning of the service. One of the inside pockets of the folder holds a registration sheet, which asks for name, address, phone number, whether member or guest, and provides a space for people to ask for more information or prayer. The other pocket holds a pencil and name tags. The worship leader encourages members and guests to fill out the registration sheet and put on a name tag. Once they fill in the information, they are invited to pass the folder down the row. This allows everyone to be noticed without standing out. The use of such a folder also helps the congregation obtain information on their first-time guests.

Smaller congregations may find this rite of friendship mundane because they all know one another. However, if the church wants to grow and reach new people, instituting this procedure will begin to create a climate of warmth. It will teach the congregation to expect guests and remind them to bring their friends. And when visitors do come, they will feel welcomed.

**6. Pick up the pace.** Today's generations have been raised on fast-paced TV—the average shot is held for seven seconds. Commercials now last fifteen to thirty seconds. This pace has shortened attention spans, but many congregations fail to recognize the new environment. The service drags on and on. Myriad dead spots litter the worship experience: The congregation finishes singing the hymn . . . the pastor walks up to the pulpit . . . she waits for the mike to come on . . . she tells the congregation to be seated . . . she prays . . . she sits down . . . the choir director stands . . . he has the choir stand . . . they open their music . . . they adjust their robes . . . the choir director raises his arms and looks at the organist . . . she asks what song they are doing . . . the choir director tells her . . . she finds the page . . . and on . . . and on . . . and on . . . .

Whenever a dead spot hits TV or radio, most people change channels or stations. In church, they cannot flip the remote control button, but they can turn off their minds.

Worship leaders can pick up the pace without making the worship experience seem rushed. Example:

As the congregation sings the final few words of the hymn, the pastor moves to the pulpit, ready to pray. While the pastor prays, the choir prepares to sing. The moment the pastor says, "Amen," they begin.

One church needed to shorten its services by several minutes. The leaders cut most of those minutes by eliminating the dead spots. With very few changes in the actual service format, they removed the dead air and improved the pace of the service.

**7. Make the service visitor-friendly.** People raised in liturgically oriented congregations can breeze through the liturgy without cracking the hymnal. The liturgy is a part of their mental wiring.

People who have never been through a liturgical service, however, often find the experience frustrating. They need help in finding their way through it. Congregations willing to provide that help send newcomers a message of acceptance. As with a visitor-friendly campus, visitor-friendly worship services help guests feel welcome.

One way to help guests through the liturgy maze is to announce everything. Tell the congregation when to stand or sit. Announce hymn numbers. Direct attention to the pew racks, where people can find the worship book or Bible. Lead the service in such a way that worshipers do not need their bulletins.

Another way to accomplish the same result: Print the entire service—liturgy, hymns, and Scripture—in the bulletin. This eliminates the frustration of turning from bulletin to hymnal to Bible to bulletin to hymnal. Before using that approach, check with your religious publishing house for permission to use copyrighted materials.

**8. Occasionally, use contemporary music.** Some contemporary styles of music fit very nicely into liturgical formats. Moving in this direction, however, requires wisdom and sensitivity. A driving rock number in a classically oriented service, for example, almost surely will alienate people. The music should be carefully chosen and appropriate to the style of the service.

Several Christian artists have written and/or recorded contemporary songs compatible with liturgical services: Sandi Patti, Steve Green, and Larnelle Harris, for instance. Contemporary music can add intimacy and the relational aspects of faith that today's consumers value.

**9. Pick singable hymns.** Unsingable hymns, like unsingable liturgy, will frustrate people and turn them off. Inspiring, celebratory hymns give the service energy. Hymns that offer an easy-to-learn melody encourage participation. The members of a Lincoln, Nebraska, congregation have purposely added a "monotone" to their worship committee. This person has veto power over any hymns he cannot sing. He represents the people in the pews who are not musically trained, a growing segment of our society.

Watch out for religious phrases in hymns. "A bulwark never failing . . . "—what does that mean? "Cherubim and Seraphim, bowing down before him . . . "—are these names of football teams? A short explanation of the meaning of words can lead to a more positive worship experience.

**10. Augment the formal prayers of the church with more informal, relational prayers.** Formal prayers can be powerful. An overdose, however, can make Christianity seem stale and lifeless. Informal "heart" prayers have a way of meeting the need for intimacy that people seek in their relationship with God.

**11. Simplify the service.** Complicated services lose their power. Worship planners attempting to make the service more dynamic will remove as much clutter as possible. They keep in mind this rule: The simpler the better. They also realize that simplifying the service takes advance planning.

Too often, because of the failure to plan, everything will be scheduled on the same Sunday: communion, confirmation, three baptisms, and a stewardship talk. The service features so many special events that none of them seems special. In another variation of that mistake, some churches with multiple services tend to put all the "stuff" at the last service. During that final service, the pastor shares the entire message. The soloist takes a few extra minutes to introduce the song. Baptisms and other religious rites are celebrated. Thus, the last service notoriously lasts too long. Which service usually has the most visitors? The last one—giving the largest numbers of guests a bad first impression!

What is the purpose of Sunday morning services? Is it to worship God, inspire believers, and introduce seekers to Jesus Christ? If so, should not anything that detracts from that purpose be reevaluated or moved to another time?

**12. Make it the best it can be.** People value quality. If it looks like junk and sounds like junk, they will assume it is junk. God is a God of excellence. Worship should always reflect that excellence. Improve the quality of the service by using literate Scripture readers, worship leaders who are comfortable praying in public, and musicians with strong musical talent.

**13. Move the altar so that the pastor faces the people.** The church I attended as a child had an altar built into the front wall of the sanctuary. Every time the pastor turned to the altar, his back was to us. I eventually came to understand the purpose behind such a design: It enabled the pastor to be a part of the worshiping community; he not only led the congregation in worship, he worshiped as one of us. Sadly, much of that symbolism is now lost. For the unchurched, it has no meaning at all.

Years ago, radio created an audio society. People listened to the radio and found their imaginations ignited, but the advent of TV and movies changed all that; the audio society became a visual society. Today, we not only listen to the action—we see

47

it. When the congregation sees only the pastor's back, a barrier is erected. People want to *hear* and *see* the pastor.

**14. Move the musicians up front.** At mid-century, many churches, fueled by an audio-orientation to participation, planted the choir loft and the organ in the back of the sanctuary. This allowed the music to minister to worshipers without the musicians "getting in the way."

Worshiping in these sanctuaries today provides an interesting insight. Because we are now a visual society, many people turn their heads to see the musicians when the music starts. Thus, putting the choir up front augments the presentation rather than detracting from it. The joyful facial expressions and enthusiasm of the choir members add to the spiritual experience. It touches more of our God-given senses.

**15. Use celebrative preludes.** Music in minor keys depresses the emotions. Use of major keys during the prelude sets a positive climate of anticipation.

Celebrative preludes also serve to eliminate the deafening silence that today's generations find uncomfortable. The days of churchgoers listening quietly to preludes are almost over. People who crave intimacy want to talk before worship. They prepare for the worship experience through conversation and relationship building. Silent contemplation intimidates and distracts them, especially if they are newcomers. Preludes, played underneath conversation, set an expectant, warm mood.

**16. Provide a quality nursery.** As with everything else, people expect the best in nursery care. If children have a bad experience in the nursery while mom and/or dad worship, the family will not return. Therefore, excellence in child care is essential to the overall success of the worship service.

That means a clean nursery. Old beat-up toys, dirty carpeting, and stained crib sheets devalue children and turn off their parents. One way to provide quality toys and furnishings is to hold a yearly nursery shower. Make up a list of nursery needs and encourage members to donate an item or two.

The primary nursery attendant should be a responsible adult, not an enthusiastic teenager. Although teenagers do make excellent assistants, parents feel much more comfortable when they know that an adult is in charge of watching their child. It is usually necessary to pay the supervising nursery attendant; this also allows you to require excellence.

**17. Warm up the sanctuary.** People enjoy the comfort of their home, and they look for that same homey feeling in church. Warm, inviting sanctuaries put people at ease as they worship. Comfortable padded pews, appropriate drapery, and well-made banners enhance the worship experience for visitors and members alike. Taking a cue from the restaurants, some newer structures even have built-in preschooler seats, equipped with trays and crayons.

Climate control also adds to or detracts from the worship experience. A hot, stuffy sanctuary or a cold, chilly sanctuary distracts people. A comfortable climate, along with a homey feel, encourages people to relax and soak in the service.

A great number of people—people who matter to God—continue to value liturgical worship, but several barriers inherent in such services keep others away. And these people also matter to God. With the suggestions outlined here and some ideas of your own, your liturgical worship can become more relevant and inviting—visitor-friendly.

However, no matter what improvements we make, liturgical worship will not be the worship of choice for some, since many are turned off by its drawbacks. Reaching new generations will require innovative forms of worship, services designed to specifically target contemporary, irreligious people.

*"I have become all things to all people,*
*that I might by all means save some."*
I Corinthians 9:22*b*

# IV

# CONTEMPORARY WORSHIP: LAYING THE FOUNDATION

Several years ago, my two children received an invitation to attend a softball game with some friends. While riding home, the friends' mom, whom I will call Kathy, asked my kids what I did for a living. When she learned that I was a pastor, she confessed that her family never attended church while she was growing up. She deeply regretted it, along with the fact that her children were not baptized.

My son Michael, seven years old at the time, said to her, "Baptism isn't all that important. It's just a little water on your head. What's important is that Jesus lives in your heart." (For all of you sacramentalists, I promise to work on his theology. However, I was very proud of him and told him he was right on.) Michael's simple expression of faith touched Kathy's heart. In fact, it so moved her that she began to weep. Moments after dropping off our kids, she called to ask about our Sunday service times.

The following week, Kathy and her family visited our church for the first time. I remember being very aware of their presence during the service. I wondered if they were following the action, if we were communicating clearly, whether we had erected any barriers that would distract them from the experience. Thankfully, they enjoyed the service and eventually joined the church. They rarely miss a Sunday.

What kind of service does a person like Kathy need the first time she comes to church? What style of worship will speak to her relevantly? How can a congregation help her overcome the confusing rituals and jargon she does not understand? What kind of service will capture her attention and move her to Jesus Christ?

## New Worship Styles for New People

Attracting people who have been turned off by the church or are unfamiliar with our styles of worship means making dramatic changes. Congregations eager to reach the millions of people like Kathy will find creative ways to take up that challenge. Instead of driving guests away with unintelligible services, outreach-oriented churches turn to alternative worship experiences by designing and implementing innovative services that cater to the needs of their guests. Contemporary worship is today's method for reaching new people.

Implementing a contemporary service, however, does not mean we must drop traditional liturgical services. Darlene Muschett, pastor of Christ the Good Shepherd in Rochester, New York, strongly cautions against such a move: "Don't take anything away. Don't pull the rug out from under the traditional members." Alternative contemporary services should supplement liturgical settings, not displace them.

Adding a new style of worship to the Sunday "menu" offers consumers a choice, and the result is often new members. Church Growth, Inc., says that almost 80 percent of all churches grow in attendance and membership when they add another worship service. The odds favor those that expand their worship schedule.

## *Five Contrasts for Designing a Contemporary Service*

Designing a contemporary service calls leaders to consider five important contrasts, or tensions:

### 1. Style Versus Substance

Many Protestant congregations tend to confuse worship styles with the substance of faith. They mistake the package for the content. Some congregations, choosing not to use the official denominational hymnal, receive criticism from their denominational family. They find themselves accused of not being Lutheran or Methodist because they offer alternative worship services. That kind of criticism implies that a particular style of worship makes a congregation uniquely Lutheran or Methodist.

Worship styles, however, do not make a congregation or its members Episcopalian, Baptist, or Catholic. Congregations demonstrate their denominational affiliation through the substance of their faith and through their commitment to work toward common purposes. Their unique understanding of the gospel makes their people Lutheran, Presbyterian, or Covenant. The theological understanding of grace, justification, the Word, and the sacraments shapes the substance of their faith, which does not change unless their doctrinal teachings change.

Worship styles, on the other hand, *communicate* the substance of faith. Styles do and must change to be relevant. Lutheran styles of worship, like those in other mainline denominations, have changed over the last five hundred years, and will continue to do so.

Many believers find the denominational styles of worship with which they grew up beautiful, meaningful, and moving. Yet these styles often fail to effectively communicate the substance of faith to those outside the church. Offering new worship experiences, without compromising the substance of faith, enables congregations to reach those "outsiders." A Juneau, Alaska, pastor came to that realization one Easter:

> We had wonderful crowds who came. I knew very well that most of the newcomers would not be back until Christmas or next

55

Easter—because our services do not draw people back. Yet I found another part of myself assuming that the services ought to bring them back. What's the point of the service, if it doesn't motivate people to return?

Few leaders would suggest using a North American denominational hymnal when planting a church in Africa or Mexico. Such services would only erect barriers to effective outreach. The language and styles of worship would be culturally irrelevant and religiously unintelligible. Instead, missionaries need the freedom to develop styles of worship that grow out of the needs of the people. One of the largest mission fields in the world is right here in the USA. Yet many insist that congregations should continue to use traditional styles of worship in speaking to today's culture. The problem: Today's unchurched culture does not understand liturgical styles of worship—and cannot comprehend the gospel through them.

A missionary mindset will help us see unreached people in a new light. Our eyes will be opened to their needs, motivating us to meet them where they are. We will discover a new willingness for developing innovative styles of worship, styles that enable us to effectively communicate the substance of our faith to the unchurched.

Bob Orr tells of a time in Martin Luther's life when he was writing new liturgies.[1] Many of Luther's followers asked for copies for use in their churches. Luther refused to share his liturgies, saying, "You know your people. Write your own liturgies." That principle still holds true. Worship is the heart-language of the people. The heart-language of those born after 1946 is different from that of previous generations. Creative, contemporary styles of worship are essential if we want to reach new generations for Jesus Christ. The decision to offer new, contemporary services is not so much a worship issue as an evangelistic issue.

## 2. Believer-oriented Versus Visitor-oriented Worship
Depending upon the audience a congregation wants to reach, worship will be shaped around one of the following three different philosophies.

One approach is *believer-oriented worship,* found in the over-whelming majority of churches across this country and the world. The primary audience is the faithful, those who know and worship God. Worship is seen as the response of God's people to God's love and grace. Believers and their needs are the focus. They set the worship agenda.

A second philosophy is *believer-oriented worship made visitor-friendly.* Churches using this approach recognize that the over-whelming majority of their worshiping audience are believers. The style of the service and the content of the sermons, there-fore, caters to them. However, the congregation goes out of its way to make sure that guests feel welcome. An atmosphere of warmth and acceptance puts visitors at ease. The service for-mat is intentionally designed to be easy to follow. (The sugges-tions outlined in the chapter on liturgical worship apply to this philosophy.)

Still another approach is *visitor-oriented worship.* Used by a growing number of churches very successfully, this is the most radical kind of worship experience. Churches that offer visi-tor-oriented worship understand the guest to be an unchurched, irreligious person. Willow Creek Community Church, in a suburb northwest of Chicago, refers to this person as a "seeker." These guests make up the target audience, and their needs shape the entire service. The music, the message, the dramas, and so on, cater to people who have never been to church before. Many believers attend this kind of service and find themselves moved by the Spirit of God. However, the needs of the first-time guest set the worship agenda—not the needs of believers. Sunday morning becomes the hook for attracting, reaching, and keeping new people.

Assuming the guest to be an unchurched person, or seeker, is the crucial element in designing this type of service. A "contemporary" service is not necessarily an outreach-oriented service. The target audience is the difference. The needs of seekers shape a vastly different kind of service than do the needs of believers.

Because of this unique approach to worship, visitor-oriented churches augment their services with aggressive dis-cipleship programs, programs designed to move people from spectators to active participants in the faith. To reel them in and hook them, visitor-oriented churches use worship as an evangelistic opportunity. Once hooked, newcomers are invited to grow through small groups, classes, retreats, and other worship opportunities. Churches like Willow Creek, Saddleback Valley, and Community Church of Joy have designed effective strategies that help their people move from being seekers to being devoted followers of Jesus Christ. The goal of these congregations is to help irreligious, nonchurched people become responsible members of the church.

Visitor-oriented congregations offer some of the best discipleship programs in the country. They produce active and committed members. The reason: A different set of expectations. Visitor-oriented churches expect their people to grow in their faith at times other than during the Sunday morning service. Sunday morning worship is not seen as a time for growth and maturity. Inspiration, encouragement, and evangelism set the priorities for the service. Growth takes an extra commitment, and visitor-oriented churches provide all kinds of opportunities for people to grow during the week.

### 3. Presentation Versus Participation

Churched people and unchurched people come to church with different expectations. Churched people come to participate in the service. They come to worship.

Guests, or seekers, come to check things out. They come to observe. They come asking, "Is this is a place where I can feel comfortable? Will my needs be met here? Is something relevant shared that I can take home with me?"

Guests do not know our songs, hymns, or creeds. They do not know when to stand or sit. So they come to watch. A visitor-oriented service responds to this dynamic by becoming highly presentational. The service intentionally limits congregational participation while heightening the presentation of the gospel. Most of the action takes place on stage, not in the pews.

The goal is to create a worship experience in which guests can understand the Savior without first needing to understand the service. Driven by that goal, the gospel is presented through several different vehicles during the service: special music (solos, ensembles, choirs, etc.), dramas, guest interviews, and the message. Sharing the gospel relevantly undergirds all the features of the service. Again, the unchurched guest sets the agenda.

Because these services focus on guests, seeker-oriented congregations often offer a believer-oriented, highly participational service during the week, perhaps on Sunday or Wednesday night. Because the unchurched set the agenda for the Sunday morning services, a believer-driven service becomes essential. These churches know that learning to worship is as important as learning to tithe, pray, and reach out to others.

One member of a seeker-oriented, presentational church questioned the need for an additional mid-week service. She felt that she participated in the weekend services, making the mid-week service unnecessary. When asked what she did during the service, how she actually participated, she said, "Well, I sing the first chorus . . . ." After a long pause, she continued, "I guess I don't really do much in the service, do I?" She began to understand the need for an additional believer-oriented service.

She then added an illuminating insight on presentational worship: "But I feel as though I participate. Through the laughter and the moving, inspirational music, the occasional tears, the dramas, and the messages that speak to where I am in my life, I feel as if I'm drawn into the action." She was speaking for many others. Even though visitor-oriented services focus on seekers, something powerful also happens in the lives of believers. Whenever the gospel is proclaimed, the Spirit of God is present and working. Through the presentation, the Spirit touches the spirits of both believers and seekers, drawing them into the action. In other words, visitor-oriented services can be believer-friendly. But to reach its target audience, visitor-oriented services will err on the side of presentation.

### 4. Cerebral Versus Celebration
Rick Warren, senior pastor of Saddleback Valley Community Church, observes that liturgical denominations have a

heavy European/East Coast influence, making them highly formal and cerebral. These traditions tend to view emotions as suspect. Christian faith is understood as an intellectual assent based on God's faithfulness, rather than an emotional feeling of security or well-being enhanced by the presence of God. As a result, worship and preaching in liturgical churches tend toward a cerebral orientation. The West Coast, on the other hand, is highly influenced by the Hispanic culture. Hispanics tend to be more celebration-oriented. In the Southeast, the same orientation among African Americans has influenced an emphasis on celebration. Today, all across North America, seekers want both celebration and information.

As discussed in the first chapter, those born after 1946 crave experiences. They hunger for a personal, dynamic encounter with God. Unfortunately, in the 1960s and 1970s, many establishment churches reacted negatively to this experiential faith. As young people searched for an experience of God, churches grew more rational in their faith approach. Worship services became more formal and structured, almost devoid of emotion. The liturgical renewal which spread throughout mainline denominations, rather than bringing contemporary worship, brought a renewed commitment to the traditional.

Not finding a vibrant, living, relevant faith in the worship or programming life of many denominational congregations, young people dropped out in record numbers. (Of the 75 million people born between 1946 and 1964, almost 50 million dropped out of church.) They were not rejecting God or faith. Their interest in faith issues remained high. Instead, they rejected what they considered to be "lifeless" religion. They rejected stale churches.

As middle-aged adults, their interest in spirituality continues to be high. Many are satisfying that interest by returning to traditional liturgical congregations. But many others, still eager to give the church a new look, crave dynamic, vibrant, personal, experiential worship. They value emotionally moving services and intellectually challenging messages. For whatever reason, liturgical worship does not speak to them. To reach them, congregations need to create a new kind of worship experience. Visitor-oriented congregations can connect with these people by using a balance of celebration and cerebral worship, addressing all facets of our God-given personalities.

## 5. Intimacy Versus Awe

Those born between 1946 and 1964 shared life with 75 million cohorts. As babies, their numbers overwhelmed hospitals. As students, they flooded grade-school classrooms and college dorms. They are now piling into an oversaturated job market. Because of their massive numbers they hunger for intimacy. They want to be known personally and to know personally. The next population wave—the 48 million people born after 1964—live in the shadow of this large generation. They too crave intimacy. They, too, want to be acknowledged and known.

In their search for intimacy, these two generations have dropped labels. If, when I was young, I called my mom's friends by their first names, she was horrified. Today my children's friends call me "Pastor Tim" or "Tim," not "Reverend Wright." They and their parents value that personal touch. In the same way, today's worshipers want a strong relational aspect in their faith and worship. They desire worship services that inspire intimacy with God.

Liturgical worship services and classical music inspire awe, moving us with the majesty and power of God. They make us aware of God's universality and grandeur. Contemporary services, on the other hand, make worship more personal. Contemporary music and worship speak the language of the heart; consequently, they move worshipers toward intimacy. It is much easier for contemporary music to move people toward awe than for classical music and liturgical worship to move them toward intimacy.

Focusing on Jesus, rather than on the first person of the Trinity, also fosters intimacy in worship. For many, God is an impersonal concept, like the Force from *Star Wars*. Jesus makes God personal and knowable. He enables us to experience intimacy with God the creator.

A COMMUNITY OF JOY

## *The Purpose of Contemporary Worship*

The purpose of liturgical worship is to lead believers into worship. Liturgical worship provides a vehicle through which believers can express their praises to God. A contemporary, visitor-oriented service has a much different purpose. It seeks to accomplish the following five things.

**1. Put the guest at ease.** Several years ago, I was standing in the back of our sanctuary when a tall, lanky young man approached me. He was visibly shaking and appeared troubled. I anticipated an emergency counseling situation. Instead, he inquired about weddings. He asked if he could be married in our church, even though he was not a member. We talked details for a few moments, and then he said, "Please forgive my shaking. I've never been in a church before, and I'm a little nervous."

Seekers often enter our churches feeling the same way. They do not know what to expect. They are apprehensive, if not actually freightened. I am unsure what they think will happen to them, but whatever it is, they think it could be awful. Visitor-oriented congregations take those feelings seriously and design services that put guests at ease. An informal setting encourages visitors to settle in and relax. An upbeat, celebratory climate, friendly people, and enthusiastic music help guests forget their fears.

**2. Eliminate religious barriers.** "Religiosity" unnerves guests. Music, dress, and symbols which hold value for believers confuse and put off younger guests. They feel as if they are walking into a foreign country. Visitor-oriented services go out of the way to remove barriers that may be confusing to the nonreligious.

**3. Introduce guests to Jesus.** The primary purpose of the visitor-oriented worship experience is to introduce irreligious people to Jesus Christ. Congregations that use this philosophy of worship make an important assumption each week: Some of the people who will attend do not have a relationship with Jesus Christ. These guests come seeking answers to life's questions. They come looking for hope. Visitor-oriented services

62

use the worship experience to share Christ in several different ways. The Good News is relevantly conveyed through music, dramas, interviews, and the message. Because Willow Creek Community Church takes this outreach aspect so seriously, its leaders do not refer to the weekend services as "worship." That takes place during the mid-week services. On the weekends, they focus on *evangelism*.

**4. Inspire and encourage believers and guests.** Proclaiming the gospel can encourage believers in their faith, and, at the same time introduce guests to Christ. Leaders of visitor-oriented worship understand how to attain the balance needed to do both.

**5. Provide a place where believers can bring their unchurched friends.** Members of congregations that offer visitor-oriented services know that they can bring their friends to worship. They feel sure their friends will be treated like royalty. Guests will not feel put down, nor will they be confused. Word of mouth is the best form of advertising, and the nonthreatening atmosphere of visitor-oriented worship gives God's people the chance to put the Great Commission into action.

With the foundation for contemporary worship poured and set, the adventure of designing and implementing the service now begins.

*"No one sews a piece of unshrunk cloth on an old cloak,*
*for the patch pulls away from the cloak,*
*and a worse tear is made.*
*Neither is new wine put into old wineskins;*
*otherwise, the skins burst,*
*and the wine is spilled,*
*and the skins are destroyed;*
*but new wine is put into fresh wineskins,*
*and so both are preserved."*

Matthew 9:16-17

# V

# DESIGNING A CONTEMPORARY OUTREACH-ORIENTED SERVICE

We launched a new visitor-driven contemporary worship service at 11:00 A.M. Easter Sunday. Ninety-five people attended. Since then, 25 percent of the worshipers have been new people. Our average attendance for all services is up 11 percent for the seven weeks after Easter. An even greater change is our shift from a maintenance mentality to a mission focus. Even people who prefer our more traditional 9:30 A.M. service see the need for and support this new mission to others. Another benefit is the personal renewal I and others have experienced as we lead this new venture.

This New York congregation has discovered what many others have learned. Outreach-oriented worship is not just more work; it brings joy, increased overall church attendance, and ignites the enthusiasm of the members about mission.

A COMMUNITY OF JOY

## Keys to Building a Contemporary
### Visitor-oriented Service

Many of the suggestions for warming up liturgical worship apply to contemporary worship as well. Implementing those ideas, along with the following suggestions, leads to more effective contemporary services.

**1. Make it contemporary.** "Different from the other service" is not sufficient. *Contemporary* implies up-to-date and relevant, and no other ingredient shapes the relevancy of a service more than the choice of music. The music used should reflect the styles of music heard on the radio *today*.

Contemporary Christian music, an ever-expanding field in the music industry, offers an invaluable tool for outreach-oriented worship. The music is sophisticated, current, and theologically sound. Stylistically, contemporary Christian music resembles the music played on "secular" radio stations. Lyrically, the words focus on Jesus. From solos to choir anthems, from worship choruses to instrumentals, from country to pop to heavy metal to inspirational to rap, contemporary Christian music offers congregations what they need to become current musically. These resources are available through most Christian bookstores.

Many congregations turn to folk services in their efforts to implement contemporary worship. Folk services, however, are no longer contemporary; they originated thirty to forty years ago and do not reach today's customer on a consistent basis. Even the name *folk* conjures up pictures of people and styles from years long ago. (And remember, today's consumers view ancient history in terms of decades, not centuries.) An occasional folk-oriented song can be used quite effectively during contemporary worship, but building a service around that style will result in frustration and disappointment. A contemporary service requires up-to-date music. In today's world, relevant, contemporary music equals a relevant, contemporary message. Older forms of music send an antique, out-of-date message.

Another factor in making worship contemporary is the "climate" or "feel" of the service. Contemporary services set a

68

relaxed and accepting environment, conveying a "come as you are" atmosphere. They emphasize the relational and lean more toward the informal. Informality does not mean sloppy or unplanned. Rather, it implies the ability to build a sense of intimacy in the worshipers.

Contemporary worship breaks down barriers through a warm, inviting climate. The informality of the service takes its cue from the surrounding culture. For example, I wear white atheletic shoes at our weekend services. Many have commented that upon seeing my shoes, they knew they had found a church home. (I call these shoes my "soul winners"—having my feet shod with the Good News of the gospel.) On the surface, this attraction to informality may not seem like a deeply spiritual reason for choosing a church. A deeper look, however, reveals an underlying attitude that guests carry with them into the service. People value acceptance and warmth. My shoes subtly tell them they can come to our church and feel comfortable. If the pastor can wear athletic shoes to worship, the people can come as they are. They need not be well-dressed or problem-free. They can carry their life's baggage into church and be welcomed. They can bring the dirty laundry of their lives and be accepted. They can relax.

The attire of the pastor and service leaders should reflect the feel of the service. Liturgical garments do not mix well with contemporary services. Even clerical collars can create a barrier. They erect an obstacle to establishing the intimacy and relationships people want and need. A casual dress, or sportcoat and tie, will help people relate more easily to the pastor. In Phoenix, following the lead of California, dress is quite informal. A sweater or a shirt and tie keep me comfortable and the service casual. The culture of the area and the target audience determines appropriate dress. If I were in the Midwest, for example, I would dress differently. Because the culture is more conservative there, I might wear a suit . . . and my black athletic shoes.

Climate and musical styles make or break the effectiveness of a contemporary service. Successful services strategically combine a relaxed, informal, relational climate with culturally current musical styles.

**2. Offer the service weekly.** Many contemporary services fail because they are offered irregularly—perhaps once or twice a month. With that kind of schedule, everyone ends up frustrated and upset. People who value liturgical worship skip those one or two Sundays when the format is contemporary. Those who enjoy contemporary worship tend to stay home on liturgical Sundays. Guests end up confused. Impressed by the contemporary service, they return the following week for more, but what they get (the liturgical service) differs so radically from the previous Sunday, they wonder if they are in the wrong church.

Whether liturgical or contemporary, services function best when offered weekly. Service formats offered once a month encourage people into either a once-a-month habit—or a consistently absent habit.

**3. Schedule the contemporary service for a later time.** Some church planners suggest that from nine to eleven on Sunday morning is the prime time for worship. If choosing between an early contemporary service or a later one, seriously consider the later option. Though it may differ in some parts of the country, later still seems a safer bet.

Believers know on Monday that they will be attending worship the following Sunday. Guests often do not decide whether to attend church until Sunday morning. If they feel like visiting a congregation that day, they will. Since they make their decision so late in the morning, they end up at the later service, so that is the service that should be geared toward them.

**4. Use the highest quality music.** If the music or message sounds like junk, guests will assume the church is junk. If the service is sloppy and unplanned, they will assume the congregation does not have its act together. People demand and expect high-quality music. God is a God of excellence. Our praise to God should be the best it can be.

I heard an old story about a church staff meeting in which the senior pastor, the associate pastor, and the minister of music had gathered for prayer. The senior pastor suggested they try something different and chant their prayers. So the senior pastor began (you can chant to yourself to make the story more enjoyable): "Lord, I'm only making $30,000 a year, and I can't live on that."

Next came the associate: "Lord, I'm only making $20,000 a year, and I can't live on that."

Then the minister of music chanted: "Lord, I'm making $50,000 a year. And there's no business like show business . . . ."

Today's worshipers see music as the most important part of the worship service. No other communication tool has more impact on these new church shoppers. Because the goal of visitor-oriented worship is to impress unchurched guests, high-quality musical presentations are essential. Worship leaders will use only the best musicians. And to ensure high standards and quality, many congregations are turning to auditions. Tactfully put, the gifts of some people who wish to perform in worship lie in other areas, so lovingly redirect them to their areas of giftedness, and the result will be greater effectiveness and happiness in their lives.

Instituting auditions is a highly sensitive issue. However, auditions benefit both the singer and the audience. Years ago, I was preparing to sing for a church-sponsored competition. I was working on a classical piece called "The Publican." The range was a bit high for me, but with practice I became comfortable with it (I have a huge range of four notes). I was asked to sing the song one Sunday at our early service. As we were singing the first hymn of the morning, I suddenly realized that I had a problem. In a mild panic, I turned to my mom, my accompanist for the day. I told her that the church piano was two steps higher than our piano at home. I did not think I could croak out the song. She assured me I would do fine. Moms do that.

So I sang. It would have been better if I had not. After the service the pastor said to me, "Well, I guess we all have our off days." When even the pastor cannot find something nice to say, you know you have blown it. Someone should have auditioned me in that church with that piano before I sang. I would have been spared a lot of embarrassment. And the congregation would have been spared a lot of pain!

Auditions, handled lovingly and professionally, will save the singer, the music department, and the congregation much embarrassment, and will also enhance the music program. Talented singers are drawn to high-quality programs. (Of course, while using auditions for soloists and ensembles, great music programs also provide opportunities for performing without auditions—the choir.)

One way to quickly improve the quality of music is to use prerecorded background tapes. These "tracks" contain fully orchestrated songs, taken directly from professional recordings. Talented soloists using these tapes will add an impressive, inexpensive professionalism to the service. However, use of background tapes requires a high-quality cassette player, patched into a high-quality sound system. Background tracks are available through most Christian bookstores. (For more on music resources see Appendix B.)

**5. Provide a high-quality sound system.** Unfortunately, many churches try to save money on this essential component of the worship center. Poor sound can ruin the best services. If the music or speaker cannot be heard, the quality of the content becomes irrelevant. If the microphone suddenly turns on half way through the first sentence, people become agitated. If the system continually feeds back, the effectiveness of the service plummets.

Those born after 1946 were raised on good-quality sound systems. They not only want to hear the sound; they want to feel it. They want it to enhance the presentation, not detract from it. One of the most important pieces of equipment in the sanctuary is the sound system. The financial investment will pay off in high-quality worship.

The sound system, however, is only as good as its technician and his or her musical ability. Some people work well with knobs and buttons but have no ear for music. A musician, trained to run the board, is usually more efficient than a technician who lacks musical ability. A great sound technician is worth paying!

**6. Keep the service moving.** Dead spots will kill a service by allowing attention to wander, so pacing is crucial. Eliminating dead air will keep the service energized. People reared in a media era are stimulated more by that which moves.

Pesky dead spots can be handled creatively without making the service feel rushed. Background music underneath transitions, for example, will subtly and effectively cover up dead spots. After a worship chorus, the pianist plays quietly as the pastor walks to the pulpit. After her prayer, music continues until the ensemble is ready to sing. Music during prayers and Bible readings keeps the service flowing.

Purists may charge manipulation, but "climate setting" is more accurate. Today's generations were raised on background music. For many, especially the unchurched, complete quiet is not the spiritual experience it may be for believers. Rather, silence intimidates. Silence makes people uncomfortable. Music, quietly played during periods of reflection, silent prayer, and transitions, eliminates distractions and enables people to focus.

Visitor-oriented services bring another dimension to worship that is often foreign to, and even discouraged, in typical mainline services—applause. In life, people applaud many things: thrilling sports plays, an exciting musical performance, heroes, and great accomplishments. The unchurched bring that same dynamic with them into church. Through applause, people express their appreciation of those who have touched them through the music or drama. The audience uses its applause to say, "Thanks!"

Because they see applause as honoring people instead of God, some believers find applause in worship disturbing and inappropriate. Actually, applause honors God and people. By honoring the people who share Christ with us, we honor Christ himself. The musicians and leaders have put in a lot of time and practice. They have given of themselves and *deserve* to be thanked. Through applause, we build up one another. Then too, applause helps to eliminate dead spots. Applause gives the pastor time to move to the pulpit after a solo. It offers an effective form of dead-spot busting.

The more simple the service, the better. Getting bogged down with in-house stuff loses the visitor. Closely related to this is length of the service. Because time has replaced money as a high value, a time-efficient service is imperative. Researcher George Barna underscores the value of time: " The secular world has recognized that a happy customer or employee is one whose needs have been anticipated, planned for, and met quickly and efficiently. Time is of the essence."[1] This new emphasis on time should have a strong impact on the planning of visitor-oriented worship. Starting and finishing on time values the time-oriented consumer. Quality and time management go together.

**7. Build each service around a theme.** A focus on a particular thought or theme gives cohesiveness and purpose to the service. That theme, emphasized throughout the service, gives worshipers something to take home with them. Normally, the theme will be dictated by the message. Selecting choruses, special music, and dramas to fit the message theme necessitates advance preparation. Four to six months of theme planning will enhance the overall impact of the service.

**8. Preach need-meeting messages.** People come to worship asking, "Does the gospel really work? Does it have anything practical to say to my life?" Because believers and seekers share the same struggles and concerns, need-meeting messages bridge the gap between them. (For more details on this point see the next two chapters.)

**9. Use high-quality leadership.** Excellence in worship is directly related to the excellence of the leadership. Worship leaders hold the responsibility for keeping the service flowing smoothly. They keep it moving. They sense when to repeat a chorus or when to move on. They provide much of the energy. As suggested in chapter III, use volunteers who read well. Find people who are comfortable when praying in public. Develop leaders sensitive to the pacing of the service. The quality of the service depends on the quality of the leaders.

The best leaders say little and allow people to worship in the way they feel comfortable. Encouraging people to sing louder, clap more, or raise their hands interrupts the worship experience. Some guests feel manipulated; others, if they do not want to express their worship in the ways called for by the worship leader, feel frustrated.

One way to enrich congregational participation is to utilize the sound system. One to three people singing into mikes creates a fuller sound, which encourages the audience to sing more enthusiastically. Projecting words on a screen also enhances participation.

One other leadership dynamic deserves attention: Those born after 1946 respond best to leaders their own age. Most of the musicians who lead worship with me are moving into their mid-thirties and early forties (although a "young" mid-thirties and "early forties"!). They reflect the median age of our target audience, as does their choice of music. However, these musicians work hard to find styles of music attractive to teenagers and young adults as well. Yet, some of our teens have referred to the music as "old people rock and roll." Imagine!

Dieter Zander, pastor of New Song Church in Walnut, California, says that 75 percent of the people in that congregation were born after 1964. When he describes the styles of music used in their worship services, I discover that our music is no more or less contemporary than theirs. Yet, ours is viewed as "old" by younger audiences.

When I mentioned this to him, he asked the age of our musicians. Upon hearing that they were middle-age adults, he suggested that younger audiences perceive the music to be "older" simply because of the age of the musicians. Though the music used at New Song is no more contemporary than ours, their worship leaders and musicians are in their twenties, the age of their target audience.

Can "older" pastors effectively reach and relate to younger audiences? I believe pastors can become more relevant to new generations by seeing life through the eyes of the generation they are called to reach. By speaking authentically to the issues important to that group, pastors can gain their trust. However, "older" pastors will need some help. Part of that help will come as they surround themselves with worship leaders who reflect the age of the target audience.

## *Getting Started*

Before implementing a contemporary service, several questions warrant consideration:

**1. Have we considered the cost?** Pastor Scott Cigich, in Arlington, Texas, cautions against making a major mistake in implementing a new service: Underestimating the amount of work it takes to pull off top-quality contemporary worship each week. In his church, sixteen people lead the contemporary service—compared to three for the liturgical service. Is your church committed to doing what it takes to make a contemporary service work?

**2. Who is our target?** Who do you want the service to reach? Will the service focus primarily on believers? If the focus is believers, will the service be visitor-friendly? Will the needs of the unchurched shape the worship agenda?

What age group will drive the music and climate of the service? Those age 45 to 65; age 25 to 45; age 18 to 25? The style of music and the content of the message will depend upon the age groups.

**3. What kind of service format will we use?** Will the service be heavy on congregational participation, or on presentation? Will there be a live band? Will there be a choir or ensemble? Who will lead the service? The pastor? The minister of music? An ensemble leader? A lay person?

Visits to other congregations will stimulate new ideas. Other denominations can provide new insights. God's Spirit is working there, too, and many innovative ideas may grow out of those visits. (Appendix A lists several formats for consideration.)

**4. What time will the service be?** Will it be an early service or a later service?

**5. Where will the service be held?** In some cases, the service may be better suited to the fellowship hall than the sanctuary. Some sanctuaries are not conducive to a more informal, relational service. Some have severe acoustical limitations. The right location is an important ingredient in a successful service.

The size of the worship facility also affects the climate of the service. If the room is too big—for example, 50 worshipers in a 300-seat auditorium—the service will lack energy and intimacy. A sense of failure will permeate the worshipers as they focus on all the empty seats. If the room is too small, attendance will stagnate. Once a sanctuary reaches 75 to 80 percent occupancy, attendance begins to plateau. A "full" sanctuary tells visitors there is no room for them.

**6. When will we launch our first service?** Some times of the year are better than others for introducing a new service. Fall kick-off Sunday, the Sunday after Labor Day, provides a great opportunity for introducing a new worship experience. As people get back into normal schedules, they may consider adding worship to their lives. Easter Sunday offers another opportune time to launch a new format. People are looking for a church on that particular day. Something new and fresh may keep them coming back.

**7. Will we offer Sunday school during the service?** This is not an easy question. Pros and cons can be listed for each choice. Congregations motivated by outreach, however, will do well to seriously consider offering Sunday school during worship. Unchurched people feel uncomfortable bringing their children into the service. Fearing their children may act up and embarrass them, they would much rather have them in Sunday school. If child care of some sort is not an option, they may opt to stay home.

Several years ago, a congregation was holding an Easter sunrise service at a local high school. During the message a child in the front row began to get restless. His mother, a guest, not knowing what to do, spanked him. The boy began to cry. So his mother spanked him again, telling him quite loudly, "Shut up!" The more she spanked and shushed him, the louder he got. No one was listening to the message. All eyes were on that scene in the front row. And hundreds of visitors were being distracted from hearing the gospel!

One Christmas Eve during my message, a little girl ran all the way down the center aisle. She stopped in front of me, looked up, and then ran back. She was cute the first time. By the fourth time, I was distracted, and so was the audience. I could tell that they had tuned me out. Their attention was on the little girl running up and down the aisle. Too embarrassed to do anything, her mother stood in the back, laughing uncomfortably. I was losing the battle. Our unchurched guests were missing out on the message.

The nature and clientele of visitor-oriented worship suggests the need for child care during the service. With no second chance to make a good first impression, minimizing the interruptions becomes crucial. Providing Sunday school during worship controls distractions and eliminates one excuse people use for not attending church. Such a provision relieves one more anxiety that unchurched guests have about worship, and also values their children. They come eager to hear something inspiring and life transforming without the necessity of watching kids. Once committed, these parents can take the time to teach their children how to sit in church. Until then, children can learn about Jesus in Sunday school while their parents hear of him in worship.

Scheduling Sunday school during worship offers another value: By hooking the children through an excellent program, parents are more likely to attend worship. Children will beg to go to Sunday school, bringing mom and/or dad with them. Many parents, though not involved in a church themselves, want to enroll their children in Sunday school. These parents are not likely to attend a class as their first introduction to the congregation, so a schedule that offers worship and Sunday school at separate hours creates a barrier. Their only option, while their children attend Sunday school, is an adult study of some kind. Too intimidated to visit a class, they usually choose to drop off their kids and go home. Should worship be offered *during* Sunday school, however, they may decide to visit the worship service, which they consider less threatening than a class.

### Key Personnel

Once the questions listed above are answered, finding a champion music leader becomes the focus. One pastor says that finding a contemporary music leader is the second most important priority in designing contemporary worship. (The top priority is determining the target audience.)

The worship leader will listen to, examine, and choose the appropriate music. He or she will audition musicians, schedule in singers, and assemble the small groups. The music director will run rehearsals and ensure top-quality presentations.

A good worship leader will exhibit several characteristics, some of which are especially important: talent; leadership ability; a passion for reaching new people through music and worship; an understanding of and agreement with the philosophy of the service; and a commitment to and knowledge of contemporary music.

Finding the right person will take time, patience, and prayer. Recruiting can happen within the congregation or, more often, outside of it. My first assignment at Community Church of Joy was to develop a Sunday evening believer's service. I immediately phoned my brother Jeff in Minneapolis. He had the passion and skills necessary for developing the contemporary music group I envisioned, so I invited him to join me in the adventure. Two major obstacles stood in the way. Accepting my offer meant Jeff had to move his family to Phoenix from Minneapolis. Second, I could offer him only $150 a month. I did promise, however, to help him find a full-time job somewhere, which I did.

After much prayer, he and his wife, Diane, agreed to come, and together, we recruited what is now known as The Good News Band. Some of the band members were auditioned from within the church. Others were recruited from outside the congregation through ads on Christian radio stations. (Other recruiting sources could include posters in Christian bookstores and ads in the religion or entertainment sections of newspapers.)

Many Christian contemporary musicians have no church home because most mainline congregations do not use or appreciate contemporary music. These musicians want to use their God-given gifts in serving the Lord. Contemporary churches attract contemporary musicians.

With the exception of our professional music staff, our musicians are volunteers. They receive no financial stipends for their involvement. Some congregations find small stipends necessary to ensure talented musicians. Usually, however, people who desire to use their music for Christ eagerly look for opportunities to serve. Their compensation comes from seeing people changed by the power of the gospel. Pats on the back and other demonstrations of appreciation keep musicians committed and excited.

### Set Up a Dry Run
Rehearsing the service before the first presentation can be very helpful. Running the service as if it were Sunday morning irons out the kinks and builds enthusiasm. The sound can be set and balanced. The musicians get a feel for what the service will look like. Dead spots can be eliminated and the pacing adjusted. The stage can be rearranged to maximize space. Sight lines can be checked. Stage clutter can be removed.

Asking a few members who believe in the service to observe the rehearsal will further sharpen it. Their honest critiques will save time and energy down the line. Videotaping the rehearsal will enable the participants to critique themselves.

Making the service the best it can be takes planning, practice, and prayer. Rehearsals and evaluation will ensure a quality presentation.

### Getting the Word Out
Advertising the new service to the target audience is another vital ingredient to its success. The issue of marketing techniques goes beyond the scope of this book, but I have included some resources in Appendix B. Direct mail, flyers, door-hangers, telemarketing, and radio and TV spots will go a long way in advertising your new service.

The best way to reach new people is to encourage members to invite their friends. Between 75 and 90 percent of all people who join a church do so because a friend or relative invites them. Helping members find creative ways to invite others has a twofold benefit: Worship attendance grows, and the members enthusiastically buy into the vision. Nothing excites believers more than seeing their friends meet Christ, thanks to their invitation.

### Building a Core
Starting a new service takes patience. Building a consistent base takes time. To build a core, some members might be

encouraged to make a nine-month commitment to the new service. As they invite their friends, the service begins to grow.

A wise move during the first month is to lovingly discourage the other members from attending the new service. Normal curiosity on their part will inflate attendance the first few weeks; as they return to their regular service, the rapid decline becomes demotivating. The worship leaders will be discouraged, as will the new attenders. Once momentum has kicked in, those in other services can be welcomed to check things out.

After five years of leading the Sunday night believer's service, I began to feel restless. My passion was to reach secular people by using innovative worship. I wanted a chance to design and lead such a service. The senior pastor was enthusiastic about the idea and suggested that we move the Sunday night crew to Sunday morning. He also recommended that we hold this new service in a movie theater, a neutral setting perhaps more comfortable for unchurched people.

We rented out six theaters—allowing room for nursery, Sunday school, and worship. In designing the new format, we modified the Willow Creek Community Church weekend service model. More than 275 people attended our first service. We were ecstatic. Unfortunately, most of those in attendance were members of our church who came out of curiosity. In two months we bottomed out at 35 adults. The frustration and discouragement were at times overwhelming. But we kept at it. And we began to grow. Six months after hitting bottom, we were averaging 80 worshipers and 25 Sunday schoolers at this alternate campus. The overwhelming majority of them were not previously members of our congregation.

Starting a new service calls for stick-to-it-ive-ness, or, in biblical terms, faith. But seeing it through is well worth it.

The pieces are finally coming together. The service is almost ready. One important ingredient, however, still needs attention: The Message!

*"How are they to call on one
in whom they have not believed?
And how are they to believe in one
of whom they have never heard?
And how are they to hear
without someone to proclaim him?
And how are they to proclaim him
unless they are sent?
As it is written,
'How beautiful are the feet of those
who bring good news!'"*

Romans 10:14-15

# VI

# PREACHING AND THE UNCHURCHED

Jan had been on our staff for a long time. She participated in the meetings that led to the many changes in our worship formats. She worked with us as we fine-tuned our Sunday morning philosophy. But while she understood it and supported it, she also struggled with it. Like many believers, she wondered if the Sunday morning services should cater more to the needs of Christians.

One Sunday morning while sitting up front with the choir, she saw a Mormon friend walk into the sanctuary. Jan says that her first response was to pray: "Oh, Lord, please don't let Pastor Walt preach a deep sermon this morning!"

Jan had an "Aha!" moment that day—a moment when she finally understood and embraced Community Church of Joy's philosophy with her whole heart. (Our views of worship and sermons change dramatically when we see them through the eyes of our guests!)

Pastors committed to making an impact on a secular culture face an almost overwhelming challenge in their preaching: Sharing the gospel relevantly with irreligious people, while at the same time inspiring believers. As with visitor-oriented worship services, visitor-oriented preaching focuses on the needs of those who never before have heard the gospel. Their needs shape a different kind of message from one written for believers. Knowing that my friend Kathy was in the audience Sunday morning made me think through my message. Would someone like Kathy, unfamiliar with the gospel, understand what I was trying to say? Or would she be confused?

## Know the Audience

Capturing the attention of secular people through preaching begins with knowing the people in that audience, with understanding what makes them tick. Most seminaries train pastors to write their messages by starting with the text. After studying and wrestling with the biblical passage, it can then be applied to the congregation.

Visitor-oriented messages, however, start with the needs of people, particularly seekers. After hearing, wrestling with, and studying their needs, a text can be chosen that speaks to those needs. As Rick Warren says, in preparing a message, the question is not, "What shall I preach about?" but, "To whom shall I preach?"[1]

### Characteristics of Today's Audience

Today's young and middle-age adults share several unique characteristics which make them quite different from previous generations.

**1. They do not know or understand our religious language.** Words like *justification*, *reconciliation*, *sin*, and even *grace* sound like a foreign language to irreligious people. So, to communicate the truths of the gospel relevantly, effective Christian communicators use new language.

Norman Vincent Peale tries to do this through the use of the phrase "positive thinking." In his attempt to talk about faith with those unfamiliar with it, he uses language that secular people understand. His use of "positive thinking" enables him to talk about Jesus in a relevant way to irreligious people. Robert Schuller does the same with "possibility thinking." He too wants to grab the attention of secular people. Through "possibility thinking," he communicates the truth of the gospel in words they understand. Theologian Paul Tillich suggests focusing on "unconditional acceptance." People connect with that kind of language. It gives them a touch-point with what they otherwise consider to be irrelevant babble.

What people do not understand, they turn off. What they perceive as irrelevant, they disregard. The gospel is still relevant. Communicating it relevantly by using new language will capture and hold the attention of new generations.

**2. Guilt no longer motivates them.** At various times since the Protestant Reformation, preachers have used guilt to motivate change. Heavy emphasis on the law, on human powerlessness and unworthiness, opened people up to forgiveness. In generations past, revivals spread throughout the country, spurred on by guilt-oriented sermons. Though still somewhat motivating for those raised during the Depression, guilt holds no power over new generations. Rather than motivating change, such emphasis now falls on deaf ears or turns off its listeners.

The generation born between 1946 and 1964 was raised on positive reinforcement. Instead of receiving demerits for poor behavior, their positive behavior was rewarded by parents and educators. Optimism, and a "You-can-do-it!" attitude shaped their thinking and their lives. *Failure* and *guilt* did not exist in their vocabulary. Thus, this generation sees guilt as a turn off. They do not respond to it as a motivator. They tune out guilt-oriented preaching. For them, guilt does not compute.

Those born after 1964 feel devalued. They feel abandoned and ignored. As a generation, they lack self-confidence. Guilt serves only to further alienate them. They do not need more put-downs. They need Good News.

A focus on the positives of the gospel attracts and motivates today's church shoppers. They want to hear what God is for, not what God is against. For instance, today's audience values messages on the benefits of marital faithfulness, rather than sermons condemning adultery. The gospel is Good News, and its positives encourage today's audience to change.

**3. Sin is not their issue.** Most people today do not think in terms of sin and forgiveness. They think in terms of their hurts and needs. Christians may recognize sin as the culprit behind many of those hurts and needs, and we may also understand the underlying need for forgiveness. Seekers, however, will not comprehend sin or forgiveness until they see the difference Christ makes in their hurt. Pastors who want to share a relevant gospel, therefore, shape their messages around needs. Once people hear their needs addressed, they can then embrace the truths of confession and absolution.

This is not to say that sin should never be addressed in seeker-oriented services. Ultimately, seekers must come to grips with their separateness from God and with the way they will respond to God's offer of forgiveness. Using language that unchurched people understand will not only point out their need for forgiveness, but will open their hearts to the great gift of God's unconditional acceptance.

In other words, *sin* needs to be defined for today's generations. "Falling short," "missing the mark," "taking the wrong path," "unbelief"—all good biblical explanations of sin—connect with today's listeners. They may not understand what *sin* is, but they know what it is to fall short of expectations. They know what it feels like to miss the mark. These word pictures help to communicate the need for forgiveness to a broken, alienated world.

The same is true when it comes to communicating the beauty of forgiveness. Phrases like "casting sin into the sea," "remembering it no more," "no longer counting it against us," and "the restoration of a broken relationship," help people to visualize the power and depth of forgiveness.

Again, if people sense that the church cares about them as individuals, if they sense that the church has something to say about their hurts and struggles, they will be open to hear what the church has to say about sin. As they grow in their faith through small groups, Bible studies, and other forms of worship, they can wrestle more in-depth with the concepts of sin, confession, repentance, forgiveness, and absolution.

**4. They lack hope.** As already mentioned, positive reinforcement shaped the lives and values of those born between 1946 and 1964. Parents believed that their post-World War II babies would be the best and brightest generation ever. Raised in a world of high expectations, those babies grew up believing it. They would do it all. They would earn more than mom and dad. They would recreate a better world. Their marriages would last. Their accomplishments would be limited only by the size of their imaginations. High expectations, promise, and hope characterized this generation.

Then reality hit. Wages failed to keep up with inflation. The expectation of earning more than mom and dad came crashing down. Today, the 1946–1964 generation finds that it takes two paychecks to equal the one check that families lived off of thirty years ago. The hoped-for accomplishments of eradicating poverty and disease failed to materialize. Moving up the corporate ladder became impossible due to the sheer size of the generation. Fifty to sixty percent of those from this generation who marry will go through a divorce.

Most of the dreams of these children of hope have fallen short. The generation of promise has become the generation of failed expectations. Life has not gone as planned. Emptiness has replaced their vision. And they need someone who will help them put the pieces back together. They need their hope restored, their confidence rebuilt.

Those born after 1964 also lack hope, but for different reasons. Instead of struggling with failed expectations, they seemingly lack expectations, period. Pastor Dieter Zander talks about how those born after 1964 believe they have inherited a broken world: a broken government; a broken environment; a broken economy; broken sex (due to AIDS); broken relationships; and even broken Christianity (due to televangelist scandals).[2] They feel as if the world is gearing up to punish them.

They see little hope economically or vocationally. Because of the huge generation before them, few high-level jobs exist. The post-1964 generation actually earns less than the two previous generations. A couple's two paychecks fall short of the two paychecks received by those born 1946–1964. They see little hope relationally. Broken, fractured families, abuse, and neglect shape their worldview. They see little hope spiritually. Though highly interested in spiritual matters, they feel as if the church has given up on them. With no hope for the present, they see very little hope for the future.

These two generations—one of failed expectations and one of low expectations—need a gospel of hope. They desperately want someone or something to give their lives meaning. They want relief from the emptiness and hurt. Pie-in-the-sky optimism will no longer cut it for them. They crave the life-transforming hope that only the gospel can offer, the deep-seated assurance that, ultimately, life makes sense. Jesus is in the business of putting together broken pieces. His promise of hope, offered two thousand years ago, remains valid today. Many will respond positively to that hope if churches can find a way to share it relevantly.

**5. They distrust leaders.** Vietnam; Watergate; the House banking scandals; Iran-Contra; the Congressional sex scandals; the fall of PTL; the fall of Jimmy Swaggart—today's audience has seen one leader after another let them down. Because of their past experience, people today not only listen to content, they inspect a communicator's character. Having been burned, they look for authentic leaders, men and women of integrity. They want us to not only say it, but live it. They listen to the message and ask, "Does the gospel really work? If it does, is it working in the life of the preacher?" Character matters. Today's audience values leaders who prove to be human, honest, and committed to their message.

**6. They lack direction.** The 1946–1964 generation has been on a lifelong quest for fulfillment. Their parents, the pre-World War II generation, grew up during the Depression. That period of crisis shaped their values. It focused them on jobs and money.

Unlike their parents, the post-World War II generation grew up in a period of affluence. Instead of focusing on jobs and money, they turned their attention to finding meaning in life. They looked for it in the protests of the 1960s. They sought fulfillment in the introspection of the 1970s. In the 1980s they tried to find it in consumption. But no matter where their search led, they always came away empty. Their quest for a meaningful philosophy of life will continue into the 1990s and beyond. A relevant, caring church can bring their search to an end.

The generation born after 1964 grew up in a world with no rules. Schools tried to teach "morally neutral" sex. Society moved from G-rated to R-rated movies. This post-1964 generation raised themselves on TV and video games, while mom and dad worked. Parents on the path to success had little time to give their children direction and values. Schools used them as "guinea pigs" for experimental curriculum. Much of that "innovative" curriculum failed, further robbing students of stability and direction.

On top of that, those born after 1964 grew up in a time of unprecedented choices. Overwhelmed by myriad options, they find themselves paralyzed with inaction. They seem to be wandering through life aimlessly, with little direction or purpose. They long for someone to help them find meaningful direction in life. A relevant church can assist them in their quest.

**7. They view truth as relative.** Several years ago, a couple came to see me for premarital counseling. During the course of the session, I discovered that the backgound of the bride to be was in an Eastern religion. As we talked about faith matters, I asked if she had ever considered the claims of Jesus. She said she believed him to be a great religious teacher, but nothing more.

I decided to try the "C. S. Lewis approach" with her. I pointed out that Jesus claimed to be God. If he is, then he is the only way to the Father. If he is lying, then he cannot be a great religious leader. Either he is God, the only God, or he is a fraud.

Her reply captures the essence of today's audience. She said, "What's true for you is true. What's true for me is true."

I asked how both "truths" could be true when our "truths" contradict each other.

But she held firm: "What you believe is right for you and what I believe is right for me."

Past generations believed in absolutes. They saw right as right and wrong as wrong. In some ways, that simplified the task of preaching. Proving God's Word to be truth often inspired people to accept it.

But today's generations do not believe in absolutes. Truth is viewed as relative. People no longer accept God's Word simply because someone says it is truth. The days of "God said it, I believe it, that settles it!" have passed. Confrontational arguments and attempts to prove the truth of Christianity fail to connect with today's generations. For them, experience determines truth: "If it feels good, it must be true."

In the 1970s, Debby Boone recorded "You Light Up My Life," and it remains one of the biggest hits ever in popular music. One phrase from that song summarizes the philosophy of today's audience when it comes to truth: "It can't be wrong, when it feels so right."

That experience-determined truth greatly affects preaching. Christian communicators can no longer rely on moving people to Christ by proving the truth of Christianity. Using the Bible to proclaim ultimate truth will inspire a lukewarm response, at best. Just because God says it does not mean that people will accept it as their standard for living.

In reaching today's audience, preachers will want to use the Bible, not to prove truth, but to influence people. Showing the Bible to be relevant will produce a greater response than showing it to be true. People want to know whether the Bible works in real life. Does it have something practical to say? Can it work in daily living?

In a world of no absolutes, communicators must not seek to *prove* the gospel, but to help people *experience* it. Effective preaching removes the barriers of unintelligibility and irrelevance, so that people can hear God speaking. It encourages them to consider the possibility of God. If people see that Jesus cares, if they discover that he can be experienced personally, they will accept Jesus as truth. Surrounding the message with a loving, caring congregation enhances its appeal. It is loving, caring relationships, not proof-texting and logical arguments, that can move people to the kingdom today.

**8. They value pragmatic messages.** Today's audience wants practical, teaching-oriented sermons. They value fix-it-oriented messages that can help them apply the gospel to their lives. They do not want pronouncements or judgmental statements. They want to know how the gospel can affect their lives, families, marriages, and careers. Quite simply, they want to know if and how the gospel works.

Grace-oriented preachers will find this characteristic of their audience particularly difficult. Such communicators already find repelling anything that suggests law or rule-oriented living. However, people today not only want to hear about grace; they want to experience it practically, in their everyday lives. After hearing, "Jesus loves me," they ask, "Now what? How does that love apply to my life?"

## *The Purpose of Visitor-oriented Preaching*

Preaching geared to irreligious people serves a function similar to that of seeker-oriented worship:

**1. It introduces people to Jesus Christ.** Seekers and a passion to reach them drive this kind of preaching. Messages geared to the unchurched provide a climate where people hear about Jesus in a nonthreatening way. By addressing their needs, seeker-oriented sermons encourage people to consider Jesus. Robert Schuller says that he uses the Sunday message to share a witness for Christ.

**2. It offers practical biblical help for daily living.** Moved to reach a highly pragmatic audience, visitor-oriented preaching seeks to demonstrate the relevancy of the Bible. Grace-empowered principles for daily life do more than provide help for those seeking it; they also influence and motivate people to dig deeper into the Christian faith. The more relevant the message, the more responsive the audience.

**3. It inspires and encourages both believers and nonbelievers.** Believers and seekers have the same needs. Both groups struggle with depression, divorce, stress, financial ups and downs, and so on. Need-oriented messages bridge the gap between these groups. They enable members and guests alike to receive God's gift of grace and encouragement.

## A Portrait of Today's Audience

In *How Can It Be All Right When Everything Is All Wrong?* Lewis B. Smedes gives us an insight into the people who grace our pews on Sunday morning:

> They came to my church on Sunday, ordinary people did, but I did not recognize them in the early days. I know now why I did not recognize them; I did not want them to be ordinary people. . . . I wanted them to be spiritual athletes, shoulders strong to bear the burdens of global justice that my prophetic words laid on them. But while I was offering them the precious promises and walloping them with the heroic mandates of the Word of God, many of them were secretly praying, "O God, I don't think I can get through the week—HELP ME!" What they needed beside my words was a miracle so that the door in the wall of their private too-muchness would open to the mystery of Christ. . . .
>
> Sometimes, as I sit in a pew and listen to a preacher calling the people to "let justice roll down like waters, and righteousness like a mighty stream" over the market places and council chambers of every village, or promise the abundance of joy and peace in the Spirit, I look around. And the *dramatis personae,* the characters in the churchly scenario, look like this for me:
>
> A man and woman, sitting board-straight, smiling on cue at every piece of funny piety, are hating each other for letting romance in their marriage collapse on a tiring treadmill of tasteless, but always tidy, tedium.
>
> A widow, whispering her Amens to every promise of divine providence, is frightened to death because the unkillable beast of inflation is devouring her savings.
>
> A father, the congregational model of parental firmness, is fuming in the suspicion of his own fatherly failure because he cannot stomach, much less understand, the furious antics of his slightly crazy son.
>
> An attractive young woman in the front pew is absolutely paralyzed, sure she has breast cancer.
>
> A middle-aged fellow who, with his new Mercedes, is an obvious Christian success story, is wondering when he will ever have the guts to tell his boss to take his lousy job and shove it.
>
> A Paulinely submissive wife of one of the elders is terrified because she is being pushed to face up to her closet alcoholism.
>
> Ordinary people, all of them, and there are a lot more where

they came from. What they have in common is a sense that everything is all wrong where it matters to them most. What they desperately need is a miracle of faith to know that life at the center is all right.[3]

These ordinary people sit in our churches every Sunday morning. They lack hope. They come hurting and disillusioned. They come hungering for a word or phrase that will inspire and encourage them, a word that will carry them through the week. They need Good News. They need to hear that Jesus loves them. They need to see that with him, ultimately, it is all right, even though things seem all wrong.

So how do preachers effectively communicate the gospel to these ordinary people? How do they shape their messages so that people can hear Jesus?

*For my thoughts are not your thoughts,*
*nor are your ways my ways, says the LORD. . . .*
*For as the rain and the snow come down from heaven,*
*and do not return there until they have watered the earth,*
*making it bring forth and sprout,*
*giving seed to the sower and bread to the eater,*
*so shall my word be that goes out from my mouth;*
*it shall not return to me empty,*
*but it shall accomplish that which I purpose,*
*and succeed in the thing for which I sent it.*

Isaiah 55:8, 10-11

# VII

# PREACHING TO IRRELIGIOUS PEOPLE

In her book *The Best Christmas Pageant Ever*, Barbara Robinson tells the story of an annual church Christmas program.

The action begins when the woman who usually "produces" the event breaks her leg. As a result, Grace Bradley, against her better judgment, finds herself pressed into service. Because the former director "always did it that way," Grace feels pressured to do the same. However, the Herdmans change everything. Beth Bradley, Grace's daughter and the story narrator, describes the Herdmans:

> The worst kids in the history of the world. They lied and stole and smoked cigars (even the girls) and talked dirty and hit little kids and cussed their teachers and took the name of the Lord in vain and set fire to Fred Shoemaker's old broken-down toolhouse.[1]

Those same Herdmans showed up for the first rehearsal, much to the shock of Grace and the "churched" kids. Her first encounter with these "irreligious Herdmans" provides insight into the challenge that faces preachers today. It also demonstrates the difficulty that many "churched people" have with visitor-oriented preaching.

99

Mother started to separate everyone into angels and shepherds and guests at the inn, but right away she ran into trouble.

"Who were the shepherds?" Leroy Herdman wanted to know. "Where did they come from?"

Ollie Herdman didn't even know what a shepherd was . . . or anyway, that's what he said.

"What was the inn?" Claude asked. "What's an inn?"

"It's like a motel," somebody told him, "where people go to spend the night . . ."

The thing was, the Herdmans didn't know anything about the Christmas story. They knew that Christmas was Jesus' birthday, but everything else was news to them—the shepherds, the Wise Men, the star, the stable, the crowded inn.

It was hard to believe. At least, it was hard for me to believe. . . .

Mother said she had better begin by reading the Christmas story from the Bible. This was a pain in the neck to most of us because we knew the whole thing backward and forward and never had to be told anything except who we were supposed to be, and where we were supposed to stand. . . .

The Herdmans were famous for never sitting still and never paying attention to anyone—teachers, parents (their own or anybody else's), the truant officer, the police—yet here they were, eyes glued on my mother and taking in every word.

"What's that?" they would yell whenever they didn't understand the language, and when Mother read about there being no room at the inn, Imogene's jaw dropped and she sat up in her seat.

"My God!" she said. "Not even for Jesus?". . .

"Well, now, after all," Mother explained, "nobody knew the baby was going to turn out to be Jesus."

"You said Mary knew," Ralph said. "Why didn't she tell them?"

"I would have told them!" Imogene put in. "Boy, would I have told them! What was the matter with Joseph that he didn't tell them? Her pregnant and everything," she grumbled.

"What was that they laid the baby in?" Leroy said. "That manger . . . is that like a bed? Why would they have a bed in a barn?" . . .

"What were the waddled up clothes?" Claude wanted to know.

"The what?" Mother said.

"You read about it—'she wrapped him in waddled up clothes.'"

"Swadling clothes," Mother sighed. "Long ago, people used to wrap their babies very tightly in big pieces of material, so they couldn't move around. It made the babies feel cozy and comfortable." . . .

"You mean they tied him up and put him in a feedbox?" Imogene said. "Where was the Child Welfare?"

I couldn't understand the Herdmans. You would have thought the Christmas story came right out of the FBI files, they got so involved in it—wanted a bloody end to Herod, worried about Mary having her baby in a barn, and called the Wise Men a bunch of dirty spies.

And they left the first rehearsal arguing about whether Joseph should have set fire to the inn, or just chased the innkeeper into the next county.[2]

## Keys for Effective Preaching to Irreligious People

How do Christian communicators prepare messages for someone who has never before heard the gospel? That question determines the shape of visitor-oriented sermons.

**1. Be relevant.** One of the problems with the church is that it often answers questions no one is asking. People want to know what the gospel has to say about everyday life. Effective preaching begins by speaking to people's needs: stress, grief, failure, family, jobs, and so on.

Jesus often used the people's needs and their questions as a starting point for his sermons (see Matt. 12:1-8 and chapters 24 and 25; Luke 7:36-50; 10:25-27; 11:1-13 and chapter 15; and John, chapter 4). Crowds admired him because he spoke with authority (Luke 4:31-32). Unlike the rabbis, who quoted others, Jesus spoke from the heart. He met the audience at their point of need. He was always relevant.

Careful listening will help preachers determine the concerns that people want addressed. Certain issues, such as financial management or child raising, will come up again and again.

The how-to section of a bookstore provides a great resource for relevant sermon ideas. The psychology and self-help sections prove especially helpful. Written to meet the needs of people (and to make money), the authors focus on sure-fire concerns.

George Barna, in *What Americans Believe: An Annual Survey of Values and Religious Views in the United States,* lists the top ten values of Americans (in descending order): family, health, time, friends, recreation, religion, the Bible, career, living comfortably, and money.[3] These values can shape several series of messages: a series on family; one on health; another on time management; a series on faith, and so on. Seekers and believers alike will find these value-oriented sermons helpful and relevant because they speak to the heart.

Counseling sessions also provide insights into the questions people want answered. One caution, however: Often those who seek out long-term counseling represent a minority of people—those with overwhelming hurts. It might be easy to assume that they represent the majority. Most people, however, do not hurt quite so deeply. They simply want practical, biblical suggestions for making life more manageable and livable. Too much counseling-generated preaching will ultimately lose the wider audience. Balance is the key.

**2. Dig into God's Word.** Once the topic or theme is decided upon, the biblical text can be chosen and researched. People come to church looking for a relevant message. They want that message to be based on God's Word. Again, they want to know what the Bible and the gospel have to say about everyday life. They are not looking for the latest psychological quick fix. They can get that in the bookstore or on TV. They hunger for lasting truths that can transform their lives.

The stakes are high when it comes to seeker-oriented preaching. A clear presentation of the gospel is imperative. In order to communicate the truths of the gospel in an understandable way, preachers need to have a firm grasp of the text. Effective preaching invests time in researching the text—its background, its language, and its meaning—and then trans-

PREACHING TO IRRELIGIOUS PEOPLE

lates and contextualizes it to the needs and issues of contemporary life. Solid biblical research cannot be compromised.

**3. Do not assume anything.** "Religious jargon" quickly loses irreligious people. In preparing the message, outreach-oriented communicators look for fresh new words, words the uninitiated can understand.

In quoting Scripture, it helps to give an explanation of what the words *chapter* and *verse* mean. Most secular people do not know Paul from Adam, or Matthew 16:16 from Isaiah 26:3. Throwing out names and verses only confuses people. Though seemingly redundant, it may be useful to say, "In one of the books of the Bible called Matthew, in chapter 5, verse 3, Jesus says . . . " or, "A follower of Jesus named Paul, writing in a letter to the church in Rome, says in chapter 8, verse 1 . . . ." Billy Graham often quotes Scripture by simply saying, "The Bible says . . . ." Most unchurched people do not care about the chapter or verse. Knowing that the quote comes from the Bible will satisfy them.

Though we try to remove religious jargon at Community Church of Joy, we still get caught assuming things. Every year people ask us, "What is Palm Sunday?" or "Why do we have Monday (Maundy) on a Thursday?" or "Why it is called Good Friday?"

Several years ago, a woman commented to a pastor that she did not realize that Christians have two Bibles. He asked what she meant, and she answered, "You have an Old Testament and a New Testament." We cannot assume anything. "Christianese" keeps people from hearing the Good News of Jesus.

**4. Move to more teaching-oriented messages.** Today's generations value pragmatic sermons. They want to know how to apply the gospel to their everyday lives. They not only want to hear the gospel, they want to experience it. Teaching-oriented messages satisfy that desire. Practical, need focused, learning-driven sermons put people in touch with a relevant gospel. To reach the irreligious, messages must answer these questions: "What's in it for me?" "Why?" and "How?" Practical, biblical principles for Christ-inspired living deal with these questions.

The use of outlines quickly and effectively gives the message a "teaching" feel. Filling in the blanks or listing the important points holds people's attention and also increases their learning. The 1946–1964 generation, in particular, values learning. Teaching-oriented messages will attract and hold them.

This style of preaching has one inherent danger, however: It can quickly deteriorate into "Law." When biblical principles for quality living are taught, they can become an end in themselves. If simply following certain rules leads to a better life, who needs Jesus? Teaching-oriented sermons focus on Jesus as the source of life. They point out a person's need for him. They demonstrate how Jesus can make a difference in life. Teaching-oriented messages help people learn to live by grace. They center on a relationship with Jesus, not rules for living. The principles serve as guides for helping people make their relationship with Christ practical and relevant.

**5. Write conversationally.** Most pastors write their messages in manuscript form. Unfortunately, the message, when presented, sounds like a literary work rather than a spoken message. Scripted messages, though mastered by some preachers, often tend to lack warmth and heart in the hands of most.

Russell Baker, in discussing his transition from columnist to host of "Masterpiece Theater," said, "Writing for the eye is different from writing for the ear." Learning to write conversationally warms up the message. Writing as if speaking directly to a person will enhance the presentation. Relationally oriented messages, rather than dissertations, connect with the heart.

**6. Value the audience.** The first Sunday after daylight-saving time, a congregation watched as their tired looking pastor moved into the pulpit. The pastor said, "As you all know, we lost an hour last night because of daylight-saving time. I don't know which hour you lost, but I lost the hour in which I usually write my sermon." He then stepped away from the pulpit and finished the service.

People value their time. They sacrifice at least an hour of that precious commodity each Sunday to worship and hear a message. Sloppy, ill-prepared messages devalue the audience; they communicate a lack of care on the part of the pastor. Unplanned sermons also devalue the gospel, which deserves the best presentation possible. Attention to studying for and writing the sermon not only polish the presentation, but also value the commitment the audience has made. In a society that depends so much on communication and information, each sermon must be prepared with excellence.

**7. Use plenty of eye contact.** Communication has become increasingly sophisticated and relational. The TV news anchors and politicians look directly at the audience through the camera. Through the use of teleprompters, they speak right to us, eye to eye. Seekers expect the same kind of relational communication when they come to church. They do not come to hear someone read to them. They come hoping for a conversation that will engage them and change their lives. Eye contact and a conversational style have become just as important as content. This means less reliance on a manuscript.

Many pastors see their lives pass before them when they contemplate moving away from the manuscript. In reality, such a move can be liberating and fairly painless. My friend Tom Eggum preaches from a manuscript, but he also has developed the art of eye contact. He becomes so familiar with the message that he shares long portions without referring to his notes.

Teaching-oriented sermons lend themselves well to this style of preaching. An occasional reference to the manuscript, while maintaining plenty of eye contact, gives the message a "classroom" feel.

Memorizing the message, though risky, proves most effective. If done well, a memorized sermon seemingly flows from the heart. It makes for the ultimate relational sermon.

I memorize my messages every week. On Wednesdays, I write out the sermon in manuscript form as if I were speaking it. Once I feel satisfied with it, I begin to learn it word for word, like an actor memorizing a script. I preach it to myself (in the bathroom) three to four times a day. As I do, the message becomes a part of me. It moves from my head to my heart. By becoming intimately familiar with it, it flows out conversationally. Then when I preach, I surrender my memory to God, and very rarely do I forget a point or get lost.

When I do forget, I either make a joke or punt. One Sunday I completely forgot an illustration. I started into it and blanked. I had to make it up as I went. Absolute terror coursed through my body. I remember praying, asking God to help me. I continued to create a story and it actually worked (or so I thought). Mentally, I shot up a word of thanks. After the service I told my family what had happened. My wife said she never knew, but my daughter said, "I knew something was wrong. That was the lamest story I've ever heard." So much for being quick on my feet!

Though risky to begin with, the benefits of memorizing far outway the negatives. Pastor Walt Kallestad, our senior pastor, also memorizes his sermons. Instead of learning them word for word as I do, however, he memorizes concepts and ideas. Whereas I preach the same message at each service on Sunday, Walt preaches several variations of his sermon. Point A in the first service might end up as point C in the second service. A story might be moved. An illustration may be added. Essentially, he shares the same thoughts each time.

No matter what the technique, eye contact will improve the quality of the message. It will make the sermon more relational and effective.

**8. Move away from the pulpit.** The pulpit creates a barrier. It alienates the speaker from the people. Though pulpits were established for acoustical reasons before we had amplifiers, it now establishes a wall between the leader and the people of God. Symbolically, it also emphasizes that the preacher is "above" the congregation, in wisdom and in authority, a turn-off for today's church shopper. By moving away from the pulpit, a pastor will further enhance the relational aspect of preaching.

Because I memorize my messages, I do not use a pulpit at all. I preach from the center of the stage, as close to the people as possible. Preaching from notes makes this more difficult. However, becoming familiar with the message can free the speaker to move away from the pulpit for a moment. Perhaps the speaker can make a conscious decision to tell all stories from outside the pulpit. Stepping away from and back to the pulpit helps draw people back into the action; it recaptures attention and brings a breath of fresh air to the message.

Sticking notes in a Bible will also liberate a speaker from the pulpit. These "crib notes" conveniently hidden in the Bible can be referred to as necessary. When not in use, the Bible can be held to one side. Holding a Bible also reminds people that the message is founded on God's Word.

**9. Get to the point.** George Barna makes the following comment:

> It seems that churches have had difficulty grasping the importance of the premium placed on time. How have Christian churches in America adapted to this changing context? Evidence of change is hard to find:
>
> Sermons remain in the 30- to 45-minute range, on average. This is in spite of the fact that the new communications environment recognizes people's shorter attention spans and the need for greater variety in presentational techniques.[4]

In this day of soundbytes, people can absorb more in a shorter time. They do not stay tuned-in to long messages. They want the message to make its point clearly, concisely, and quickly. This means that effective communicators learn to develop the economy of words; they say what they have to say efficiently and with the greatest possible impact. Leaving people wanting more proves better in the long run than feeling they are praying for the sermon to end. A 15- to 25-minute message is generally adequate for today's audiences.

Sometimes the sermon length depends on the pastor. A few pastors, because of their gifting, can hold the audience for longer periods of time. Some audiences—the highly educated, for example—may enjoy longer messages. On the whole, however, many people, particularly irreligious people, appreciate a well done, concise, to-the-point message.

In 1689, Dr. Robert South looked up from his sermon notes only to experience a pastor's worst nightmare. The entire congregation, including His Majesty, had fallen asleep. Embarrassed and unsure of what to do, Dr. South said, "Lord Lauderdale, rouse yourself. You snore so loudly that you will wake the king!"[5] Getting to the point will save many communicators and audiences from such embarrassment.

**10. Seek to inspire.** A Baptist pastor tells of a member who approached him after the message with this advice: "Pastor, the world beats the hell out of me all week long. I don't need you to do the same thing on Sunday morning." People come to worship looking for inspiration and encouragement. They come seeking hope. They come anxious for a word that will help them face the week ahead, that will help them make sense out of life. They do not need more bad news. They hear enough of that all week long.

Although the gospel is *Good News,* many churches communicate it in ways that sound like bad news. People walk away devalued rather than built up. They feel inadequate rather than loved. Instead of offering hope, the message pushes a certain agenda of the preacher or the denomination. The "Law," rather than the gospel, sets the tone.

Confusion over the use of law/gospel often leads to ineffective preaching. Some believe preaching the law means condemning, showing people how bad they are. Supposedly, once sufficiently convinced of their worthlessness, they will eagerly embrace the gospel. This understanding of law/gospel serves only to alienate hurting people. It beats them down to a point where they cannot hear the Good News. Condemnation turns people off. It fails to open them to Jesus.

The law aspect of preaching does not function to put people down, but to remind them of their need for Christ. It identifies with their hurts, fears, hopelessness, and their powerlessness to do anything about those problems. This creates within them a hunger for help. Having exposed the need, the gospel comes as a soothing balm—a word of hope that heals the hurt and meets the needs. In other words, law/gospel preaching is really need/gospel preaching.

People already know their inadequacies. They already know their need for something more in life. Instead of salt in their wounds, they need salve for healing. Preaching the law will not move them to change. Only the unconditional love of Jesus Christ can transform lives.

> Do not pound Christians [or anybody, for that matter] with the law in order to make them love; the law kindles no love. Set them afire in love by the love of Christ, who died for them.[6]

For the same reason, the Sunday-morning focus should always be on people, not on controversial issues. In preparing the message, preachers need to ask: "Does the message set people free? Does it offer comfort to terrorized consciences? Does it offer hope and encouragement?" Dealing with controversial issues has a place in the church. The gospel does speak to the troublesome situations of modern culture. But classroom forums which encourage discussion provide a much better setting for such topics than do sermons. In those settings, people can ask questions, seek clarification, and offer differing viewpoints. They can also pray together before leaving, reaffirming their oneness in the midst of disagreement.

Again, the audience and the purpose of the message determine the topics. Visitor-oriented services use worship and sermons to point seekers to Jesus, to inspire them with the love of Christ. Any subjects or issues that detract from this purpose can be dealt with in other settings. Sunday-morning worship should focus on inspiration. Small groups, Bible studies, and classes provide opportunities for discipleship and challenge.

**11. Use humor.** The post-1964 generation places a high premium on fun. They expect to have fun on the job, in their lives, and in church! Well placed, appropriate humor breaks down barriers and helps loosen people up. Visitors, especially those attending church for the very first time, usually arrive tense and uptight. They don't know what to expect. Many are downright afraid. Humor helps them release the nervous tension of being in church. It creates a warm, inviting climate.

After church on Sunday, several of us go out for pizza. Being regulars, we had become friends with the manager. Our friendship grew to a point where we eventually invited her to worship. She enthusiastically promised to come. One of our members arranged to meet her at a certain place before the service.

Sunday came, but we could not find her. We knew she would be there. She had given her word. But she was nowhere in sight. We finally found her hiding behind a pillar. She was too frightened to come into the sanctuary. She feared she might not be dressed right. She did not feel worthy. Having never been to church before, she felt awkward and intimidated.

Humor can help put such people at ease. It helps them settle in and relax. Opening the message with a good piece of humor captures people's attention immediately. A funny story in the middle of the message enables people to catch their breath. It draws them back into the message. Humor builds rapport between the speaker and the audience.

Of course, not every joke works, but even bombs can be great opportunities to poke fun at yourself. David Letterman masterfully uses flat jokes to his advantage.

**12. Use stories.** Stories and illustrations move the message from the head to the heart, and they also help people apply the message to their lives. Men in particular, being more visual than verbal, respond well to stories, which, generally speaking, should be contemporary and not too long. They should enhance the point being made.

**13. Be authentic.** Personal stories add instant relatability to the message. They make the preacher human and accessible. Sharing personal joys and struggles breaks down the wall between the speaker and the audience. A pastor's openness gives the people permission to deal openly with their own issues. They find encouragement in knowing that the pastor experiences life as they do. Personal stories help make the gospel more relevant and tangible.

Authenticity, though valuable, takes courage and the willingness to risk. A few years ago I did a four-week series called "Living Anxiety Free." It grew out of my own struggle with anxiety and panic attacks. On the first Sunday of the series, I shared my story.

I told of waking up at 3:00 A.M. in California, absolutely panicked. I had never been so afraid in my life, and I had no idea why. I packed up my car and, at 3:30, began the six-hour drive back to Phoenix. By the time I arrived home the panic had passed. But a year later it returned, and stayed. For several months I battled anxiety and depression.

Thankfully, through counseling and personal study I learned to manage my anxiety. In my research, I discovered that one out of every nine people in the U.S. struggles with anxiety. I figured that many in our congregation suffered just as I did, and they needed someone to tell them they were O.K., that healing was possible.

I took the risk of opening myself up and being vulnerable. During those four weeks, our attendance increased by 150 to 200 people. Anxiety sufferers came out of the woodwork. Our follow-up seminar on anxiety drew record numbers. More important, people found hope and help. My openness gave them permission to admit their hurts and struggles. It paved the way for them to seek help.

Years later, people still talk about that series. Becoming vulnerable made me more human and better able to relate to the audience. It created a new climate of openness and honesty. Many found hope in the fact that in the midst of my hurt and struggle, I still got up and preached. It gave them the assurance that they could bring their hurts and struggles with them to church. It also showed them that the gospel can make a difference.

**14. Use series.** In this day of shorter sermons, preaching a series enables pastors to more fully develop a theme, and they also make great marketing tools. If people enjoy the series, they will come back for more. They may even bring their friends along. My series on anxiety worked that way. A five- to six-week series can be a wonderful hook for attracting newcomers.

Remember, however, that on any given Sunday, many in the audience will have missed the previous week. In series preaching, then, each message in the series should be self-contained, able to stand by itself. And the entire series should not be too long, or eventually it will lose steam.

**15. Use sermon titles.** Effective titles help attract attention and prepare people to think in terms of a particular theme. Titles help reinforce the emphasis of the message. They offer a clue as to what will be discussed without giving away the whole message. They convey the sense that the message has something relevant to say. Seeker-driven messages will use visitor-friendly titles. "A New Look at Leviticus" will not cut it. But "Making Your House a Home" might.

As with series, message titles make excellent marketing tools. The titles should be exciting, practical, and relevant. (See Appendix B for suggestions.)

**16. Preach with enthusiasm.** Energetic preaching ignites people. It captures and holds their attention. An enthusiastic message equates with an exciting, dynamic gospel.

**17. Be yourself.** Pastor Luke Biggs says:

> A lot of pastors hear some great preachers (Swindoll, Hybels, Maxwell, etc.) and try to imitate them. This is a mistake. I have found that everyone has a preaching style that is unique to them. Some are didactic, some are homiletic, some are storytellers, etc. The goal is to find your best style and sharpen the skills that will help you do *that style* best. Included in these skills would be: Learning to preach "note-free" sermons. . . . Learning how to get the best out of your voice. . . . Learning to apply analytic skills to gain consistency of quality in your sermons.

In other words, be the preacher God created *you* to be!

**18. Uphold the integrity of the gospel.** Bob Parsons, pastor of Sierra Vista United Methodist Church in San Angelo, Texas, offers this summary of visitor-oriented preaching:

A. Know your people's pain.
B. Make certain they receive the healing words for their specific pains.
C. Use recognizable symbols (stories, images, parables).
D. Use theological integrity.
E. Use theological integrity.
F. Use theological integrity.

## A Deep Sermon?

Pastors committed to preaching seeker-oriented sermons may find themselves criticized occasionally by their members. From time to time, for example, believers tell us that our sermons lack depth. These well-meaning members do not feel "fed." They want "meatier" sermons. George Hunter, quoting Alan Walker, puts it this way:

> Unfortunately, as Alan Walker notes, "An idolatry of words has grown up in evangelism. There are many people, who, if they fail to hear the repetition of phrases and words with which they are familiar, make the sometimes absurd claim that the gospel is not being preached." . . .
> Your language will never "please all of the people all of the time." The language that appeals to some group in the church will miss the outsiders; the language that engages the person with no Christian memory won't sound sufficiently religious, or evangelical, or inclusive, or traditional, or avant garde, or yuppie to some insiders.[7]

Truly "deep" sermons move people with the gospel and touch them in a life-changing way. They point people to Jesus. They offer the audience practical help in living out their relationship with God. Truly "meaty" messages set people free with the gospel.

Words do not determine the depth of a message. Depth happens as the Spirit applies the message to the heart of the listener. Through the proclamation of God's Word, truth finds its level of depth; it speaks to a person at his or her point of need. George Hunter continues with this advice for minimizing misunderstanding and criticism:

> How does the apostle resolve this dilemma? By speaking for and to the unchurched, while patiently explaining to the faithful, over and over again, what one is doing as a communicator, and why, and encouraging them to do likewise![8]

113

## Getting Started

Sermons, like art, are very personal. Pastors take their messages seriously because they see the sermon as an extension of themselves. Sermons open the window to the preacher's heart. Pastors, therefore, want their messages to be the best they can be. Each pastor has a different technique and style for preparing and writing a message. The most effective preachers continue to hone and perfect their styles and techniques throughout their careers.

Listed below is one possible process for sermon development and writing:

**1. Map out the series, topics, and texts for the next four to six months.** Advance planning brings focus. It keeps pastors open to stories and ideas. For the next several months, they can think about and gather stories for upcoming messages. When it comes time to write a sermon, months of thought have already gone into it. Advance planning makes the task of preaching easier and more enjoyable.

One pastor created a "Sermon Design Team" in his congregation. This team spends months carefully listening to the struggles and needs of the churched and the unchurched. They then meet with the pastor and help to organize sermon series dealing with the needs they have uncovered.

**2. Develop a "Sermon Research Team."** Just as a "Sermon Design Team" helps choose the topics, a "Sermon Research Team" researches the topics. This group assists the pastor in finding data and stories for the message. Each team member focuses on a specific message and text. Their study and research not only save the pastor time, but fire up the researchers, as well.

Every congregation has a member or two who enjoy research. Setting these persons free to track down pertinent information and stories values them and their gifts. It also takes seriously the concept of the "priesthood of all believers."

**3. Set aside two to three hours on Monday or Tuesday for studying the text.** Digging into the text keeps pastors in touch with God's heart. Researching Greek or Hebrew words, reading commentaries, and cross-referencing other texts ensure a well-grounded message. Allowing the research to set for a day gives it a chance to shape one's thinking.

**4. Set aside two to three hours on Tuesday or Wednesday for further research and story gathering.** Stories bring life to the message. Every Sunday, I ask my wife's opinion of my sermon. She always responds by mentioning the illustration that most affected her. The point of the message gets across because a story captures her heart. Story research, therefore, deserves the same amount of time as text research. (See Appendix B for illustration resources.)

In addition to textual study and the stories, some sermon topics require additional research. Messages on stress, relationships, careers, and financial management will be greatly enhanced by reading what "experts" have to say on the subject. Using their insights, research, and statistics makes for a more relevant sermon.

**5. Set aside three to four hours on Thursday, or Friday at the latest, to write the message.** Writing the sermon several days before the presentation gives pastors a chance to "try it on." It enables them to live with it for a while before preaching it.

**6. Review the sermon two or three times a day until Sunday.** The more review, the more the sermon will flow from the heart. Continual review gives pastors confidence and also energizes the overall presentation.

**7. Commit the message to God.** All pastors have their off days. Sometimes, the normal pressures of pastoring cuts short the sermon preparation time. At other times, the best written sermons seem like burnt offerings. One week, the message may flow onto the paper (or computer) effortlessly. The next week, writer's block attacks. Thankfully, God's Word never returns empty, and once written, the sermon belongs to God. His Spirit will use it for God's honor and glory. What a relief!

The service and message are now ready. However, a few important details need some attention and fine-tuning.

*"For God so loved the world
that he gave his only Son,
so that everyone who believes in him
may not perish but may have eternal life.
Indeed, God did not send the Son into the world
to condemn the world,
but in order that the world
might be saved through him."*

John 3:16-17

# VIII
# FINE-TUNING

"You are the Christ! The Son of the Living God!"

Goosebumps raced up and down my body as Joel proclaimed those great words of faith. He was playing the part of Peter in our Maundy Thursday service. Only a few weeks earlier, Joel, born Jewish, had discovered Jesus as the Messiah.

Joel and his Protestant wife, Laury, had found this joyful church a nonthreatening place for their unique family. Through the visitor-oriented worship, he was able to hear about Jesus in a comfortable, accepting environment. After many exposures to the gospel, the love of Christ overwhelmed him and he surrendered his life to Jesus. In playing the part of Peter, Joel did more than recite a line. He gave witness to the truth he had discovered personally.

### *The Mission-driven Church*

A passion for reaching people like Joel undergirds this entire book. Christ's call to mission (Matt. 28:19-20) shapes the principles offered in these pages. Visitor-oriented services begin with a commitment to, and an understanding of that mission.

**1. Mission is not about programs. Mission is a way of programming the church.** Mission-driven congregations focus their energy on finding lost people and introducing them to Jesus Christ. They do not assign the task of mission to the evangelism committee. Instead, mission shapes the essence of what the church is all about. Mission permeates every program of the congregation.

**2. Mission is not about numbers. Mission is about people.** Tracking attendance and membership helps the congregation determine its health. Numbers provide a barometer against which the effectiveness of the mission can be measured. Numbers, however, are never recorded merely for the sake of numbers. Every statistic represents a person who needs Jesus Christ.

Pastor Walt Kallestad tells of joining his daughter on a field trip years ago. He noticed how diligently the teacher counted the students as they headed out. Before returning to the school, she again counted the students.

Walt says, "Suppose, after arriving back at school, the children climb off the bus. Eager moms and dads hug their kids and excitedly talk about the trip. However, one set of parents stands alone. They cannot find their daughter. When they ask the teacher about their child, she says, 'Well, what do you expect. I got 99 percent of them home. What's the big deal?' Numbers do matter, because every number represents a person!"

Ask the stewardship committee whether numbers matter!

Mission-oriented churches advocate growth for the sake of people. Being the largest church in the country provides little motivation. But lost people do. As long as their city has people living outside a relationship with Christ, mission-driven churches will reach out. Following Christ's lead, they will go into the world, making disciples. Mission-oriented churches grow in both quality and quantity. Numbers inspire them to be more efficient in their mission.

**3. Mission-driven congregations think unchurched.** Mission-minded congregations know that the unchurched think differently from churched people. Believers derive their values from the gospel. The unchurched derive their values from secular society. Mission-oriented congregations, therefore, seek to re-

120

interpret the gospel in language familiar to the irreligious. To reach secular people, mission-driven churches seek to understand them and think as they do.

**4. Mission-driven churches dream and plan unchurched.** The needs of the irreligious set the agenda for outreach-oriented churches. Those who do not know Jesus Christ determine the focus of the church's mission. They become the priority.

**5. Mission-driven churches create a positive climate.** Mission-oriented congregations know the life-transforming value of the Good News. They eagerly seek to share that Good News as positively as possible. They strive to set a nonthreatening climate in worship, breaking down barriers so that the irreligious can comfortably hear about Jesus. Mission-minded congregations know that a loving, warm, accepting atmosphere will encourage guests to come back again.

**6. Mission-driven congregations focus on relationships.** Mission-oriented churches see the building of relationships as the most important task of the church. Positive relationships open people up to the gospel. People, not issues, drive the mission-minded church.

## What About . . . ?

Visitor-oriented worship has a great impact on every element of the service. Several of those elements deserve special attention, especially the sacraments. Being Lutheran, I hold a high view of baptism and communion, as do most in establishment churches. The sacraments provide us with symbols of the gospel. Through them, God reaches down to us with love and grace. Baptism and communion enhance believer-oriented worship, but in a visitor-oriented service, the place of the sacraments becomes a different matter.

### Communion
Several years ago our congregation considered removing communion from the weekend services. We felt that the Lord's Supper might be too believer-oriented for a visitor-driven

service. Our plan was to offer communion exclusively at our Wednesday evening believer's service.

Through prayer and guidance from others, we finally decided against such a move. We came to realize that communion provides another way for God to communicate with us. Perhaps, through communion, a seeker might experience a life-changing encounter with Jesus Christ. If God can use music and the message to change lives, the same can be true of the Eucharist.

We strive to be clear about who should come for communion. In introducing it, we give a "disclaimer." We invite all, but ask that they have a living, personal relationship with Jesus Christ, that they truly believe he is present in the meal. Should seekers come, and some do, we believe that God can work in a life-transforming way.

Each mission-driven congregation will need to wrestle with this issue. Theology, policy, and mission will determine how and when communion will be celebrated.

Some congregations have a "closed" policy when it comes to participating in the Eucharist: Only baptized members of the congregation or denomination may receive the bread and wine. This policy will not work in a visitor-oriented service. "Excluding" guests will turn them off. It destroys the welcoming environment that the church tried to create.

Congregations with a closed policy may find it best not to offer communion during visitor-oriented services. Perhaps it can be celebrated in a side room after worship. Although members may rebel against such a move, making sure they understand the purpose behind visitor-oriented worship will keep this issue from blowing up.

Congregations with an open policy can help guests by giving detailed instructions about how to receive communion. Visitors want to know whether they should open their hand or their mouth to receive the bread. They want to know whether they should stand or kneel. Mission-driven congregations assume that some in the audience have never received the Eucharist before at their church. Walking them through the experience will make the event more meaningful.

In large congregations with several hundred people, there may not be time to serve around the altar, so many congregations serve communion at several stations across their sanctuaries. People walk forward to a server who gives them the bread (or wafer). Then they move a few steps to the person serving the wine. Having sipped the wine, they place their cup in an empty tray and return to their seats. In addition to maximizing time, this method offers two further benefits: The continual movement creates a sense of excitement and energy; and guests who choose not to participate do not feel conspicuous.

On the other hand, serving around the altar creates a sense of intimacy. The communicant experiences a deeply private moment with God, the giver of life and forgiveness. It allows a moment for prayer and reflection.

During the serving of communion, the musicians can lead the congregation in a time of singing. This helps set a mood of celebration and removes the silence that guests find intimidating.

A word about the common cup: While believers may appreciate the symbolism behind the common cup, visitors find it uncomfortable. Offering individual cups along with the common cup will put guests at ease.

### Baptism

Baptism raises at least three challenges, or questions, for visitor-oriented services.

**1. How will we keep the attention of seekers during the service of baptism?** Baptism provides a powerful witness to new life in Christ. The service itself, however, often fails to draw seekers into the action. They do not understand its significance. The rite proves unintelligible. For five or six minutes, the whole focus is on the one or two people being baptized, and since visitors have no vested interest in those people, they tune out the action. What they do not understand, they turn off. In other words, in visitor-oriented services, the rite of baptism loses the audience.

Congregations that choose to offer baptisms during visitor-oriented worship try to make them relevant for seekers. Taking a few minutes to explain the significance of baptism helps. Positioning the families so that the audience can witness the action keeps their attention. Music played underneath the rite keeps the service flowing. Warming up the language—making it relational, rather than liturgical—will make the service more meaningful.

**2. Will we baptize nonmembers?** Because of their focus, mission-driven churches attract large numbers of irreligious visitors. These unchurched people often want their children baptized, though more out of obligation than spiritual motivation. This issue poses a challenge: Will the congregation baptize children whose parents are unattached to the church?

If the answer is No, because the congregation believes that infant baptism is a covenant between the church and the family, the question then becomes: "How do we build a bridge to keep the family in touch with the church?" That question points to a great responsibility.

Many congregations answer Yes, choosing to err on the side of grace by baptizing children of unchurched families. These congregations take seriously the task of building bridges. Instead of turning people away, they seek to plant "seeds of grace" through baptism.

With this open policy, the pre-baptism class becomes crucial. This class focuses not so much on training as on building relationships. The pastor spends time getting to know the family. She or he gives an overview of the church and invites the family to worship. The pastor creates a warm, loving climate that will perhaps encourage the family to come back.

**3. Will we offer baptism during the service, or afterward?** Newcomers and guests often feel uncomfortable standing up in front of a group of strangers for baptism. The larger the congregation, the more this becomes a concern. Mission-driven churches often receive requests for private baptisms.

In response to this and the other challenges above, some congregations choose to perform baptisms after the service. The families attend worship and celebrate the baptism afterward. The down side of this decision is that it fails to capture the corporate aspect of baptism. But because of the challenges, many churches choose this route.

Again, other congregations find ways to overcome these challenges and incorporate baptism into visitor-oriented services. Each mission-driven congregation must deal with this important issue on their own.

## Confession and Absolution

As previously mentioned, irreligious people do not necessarily perceive sin as their problem. The rite of confession and absolution can come across to them as condemning. If not done with their needs and perceptions in mind, confession and absolution will alienate visitors.

Mission-driven churches seek to communicate forgiveness and acceptance throughout the worship experience. Through the proclamation of the gospel, people begin to experience release from all that binds them. Through the loving, open climate, grace and acceptance begins to permeate their lives.

Visitor-oriented worship functions as evangelism. It serves as a tool for introducing people to Jesus. Confession and absolution, then, though not done overtly, weaves itself throughout the service. An informal prayer near the beginning of the service can be used as a form of confession. A moment of silence gives people a chance to confess their shortcomings or needs to Jesus. Following up with a word of thanks to God for forgiveness and help serves as the absolution.

Closing the service or message with a time for commitment also functions as confession and forgiveness. As people surrender their lives to Christ, confession and forgiveness become a living reality for them.

Using a prewritten, formulaic liturgical prayer of confession and forgiveness in visitor-oriented services proves awkward, at best. Warming up the language, making it relational, will make the rite more relevant.

## Prayer

Visitor-oriented services provide one risk for mission-driven churches: People's lives will be changed. And they will want a way to express that change and better understand it. Providing a place for people to pray and receive counseling becomes as important as the service itself.

Many churches have a designated prayer room. Trained counselors staff the room each weekend. At the end of the service the leaders invite anyone and everyone to stop by for prayer, no matter what their need might be—a request for healing, an invitation to receive Christ, a prayer of thanksgiving, and so forth. Such an invitation reminds people that God is still alive and that God can be experienced through prayer.

### Announcements

Put delicately, worship leaders hate announcements. So does everyone else. However, announcements do affect programming. Without them, effectiveness drops dramatically. Program attendance suffers. The volunteer needs go unattended.

Corporations understand the necessity of multiple reminders. McDonald's, for example, the best known hamburger restaurant in the world, still spends millions on advertising. If people do not hear about it over and over, they forget about it. The same holds true for church programming. (Besides, how does one drop a liturgical rite that traces its history back to Moses?)

Announcements, however, quickly lose the interest of the audience. Most are "in-house," having no connection at all to the visitor. For them, this "blank spot" brings the service to a screeching halt. Therefore, in visitor-oriented services, announcements should be brief and pertinent to the whole audience. For instance, our church announces the Wednesday evening believers service, an event open to everyone. We highlight no more than two events, along with that service, keeping the announcements to two minutes.

Specialized announcements can be handled through bulletins and the welcome booth. However, watch out for the barrage of fliers. An overdose of fliers overwhelms visitors. Coordination of all advertising proves most effective in the long run.

## The Offering

Many people stay away from church because they perceive it to be money hungry. Unfortunately, the taking of an offering feeds into that perception. While believers know that the church cannot function without offerings, seekers do not. They honestly have no understanding of how a congregation funds its ministries. Many think the money comes from denominational headquarters. Many do not even think about it. They know only that the church has existed up to that point without their money. Why should they give now?

Finding creative ways to ask for money without alienating seekers poses a continual challenge for mission-driven churches. Taking up an offering (and paying the bills) without using a hard sell often proves difficult.

Willow Creek Community Church uses perhaps the most innovative approach. The worship leaders tell guests they need not give! Willow Creek wants to overcome the "money-hungry" image that seekers have of the church, so visitors are informed that it is not necessary to participate in the offering. Your church treasurer may pass out when this freedom is announced from your podium.

In visiting a church, seekers continually ask, "What's in it for me?" That question carries over into the offering: "What possible benefit might there be for me in giving away some of my hard-earned money?" Taking a moment to answer that question may not move them to give, but it may help them to see the offering and the church in a new light.

In announcing the offering, our church uses mission-oriented language. We talk about the difference our investment makes in the world. We talk about how giving benefits each person, through better programming and great worship. At times, we even remind the audience that our church functions solely on their giving. They play an important role in a great mission. Our point is not to persuade seekers to give. Like other seeker-sensitive churches, we want to break down the stereotype of a "money-hungry" church.

## The Anchors of the Faith

Those of us raised on liturgical worship often struggle with the kind of foundation provided by contemporary worship. After all, *contemporary*, by its very nature, means "temporary."

For past generations, liturgy provided the anchor that kept people grounded in the faith. It drew them back to the church week after week. It nourished and strengthened them. Though still valid for many millions of Christians, liturgical worship no longer has the same holding power for certain segments of today's unchurched population. In addition to worship, visitor-oriented churches find that other anchors must be emphasized in order to ground people in the faith: a personal, intimate relationship with Jesus Christ; a dynamic prayer life; Bible study; opportunities to put their faith into action in the world; and relationships with other believers—that is, small groups. These anchors enhance the holding power of worship.

Visitor-oriented worship draws people back week after week through inspiration and encouragement. It also encourages them to discover maturity through these other faith anchors. Though the styles of worship will change (such is the nature of contemporary worship) the anchors will remain.

While liturgical worship continues to inspire many in their praise of God, it does not have the same appeal for everyone. Many unchurched people will not be reached through traditional liturgical forms of worship. The point of this book has not been to in any way discredit liturgical worship. Rather, it has endeavored to suggest the need for alternative styles of worship, to reach those not reached through traditional forms.

## A Closing Invitation

All over the world, God is doing a new thing in the area of worship and evangelism. How might your church respond to this new adventure?

Saddle up your horses! We've got a trail to blaze. Through the wild blue yonder of God's amazing grace.[1]

*O sing to the LORD a new song;*
*sing to the LORD, all the earth.*
*Sing to the LORD, bless his name;*
*tell of his salvation from day to day.*
*Declare his glory among the nations,*
*his marvelous works among all the peoples.*
Psalm 96:1-3

# APPENDIX A
## Worship Formats

### I. Visitor-oriented, Presentational Formats

The formats in this section follow the same basic outline, with minor variations. Using a similar format week after week, while adding occasional variations, builds both familiarity and surprise. Church shoppers value both.

A word concerning preludes: Chosen carefully, preludes help to create an environment of celebration. The prelude should reflect the climate of the service. For instance, an organ prelude before a contemporary service will prove disastrous, as will a contemporary pop tape before a liturgical service. Tapes, keyboards, or a band can provide the sense of excitement necessary for a visitor-oriented, contemporary service.

* Denotes when the congregation may stand.

#### Format #1

It may be helpful to view this service as two acts: Act 1—Celebration and preparation for the message; Act 2—The message and invitation. The offering serves, in a sense, as the transition between the two acts.

*Call to Worship*—a strong, up-tempo musical number by the choir or ensemble. The call to worship sets the climate and energy level of the service.

*Welcome*—an enthusiastic welcome by the pastor to the congregation. Dr. Robert Schuller, of the Crystal Cathedral, often begins with Psalm 118:24: "This is the day that the Lord has made. Let us rejoice and be glad in it." An energetic, warm welcome continues to set a climate of expectancy. The pastor and leaders may consider introducing themselves, assuming there are visitors.

After a brief welcome, the pastor invites the congregation to greet those around them. Music can play softly in the background. After this time of greeting, the pastor might give a short overview of the theme for the day. I share a humorous anecdote if I have one, something light that helps put people at ease. The welcome folders, referred to in a previous chapter, can be handed out at this point. Invite members, as well as guests, to fill it out and put on a name tag. This will ensure a higher level of participation.

Before inviting the audience to sing, I remind them that Jesus Christ is present, that he stands ready to meet any and every need they may have.

*\*Worship Chorus*—a good contemporary, singable chorus. If the musicians sing it through first, the guests have a chance to learn the song. A talented band may lead one up-tempo chorus, following it with a more worshipful chorus.

*The Bible Reading and Prayer*—The biblical text for the morning's message is read. The reading is more relevant if the congregation is reminded of the message theme and how the text relates to it. A general prayer of welcome to God follows, inviting God to speak to us. Sometimes a moment of silence can be offered for reflection and confession (with background music). Absolution can be shared through the prayer or through proclamation.

*Special Feature*—This may be a minidrama, or skit, focusing on the message theme. Or it may be a guest interview—someone with a faith story to tell (athletes, business people, members of the congregation, etc.). An "interviewer" who asks questions about the person's life and faith journey keeps the interview moving. It also keeps the control of the service in the hands of the worship leaders. Dr. Schuller does this well. The special feature can also include a solo artist who performs a miniconcert of two or three songs.

*Special Music*—a number by the band, soloist or choir.

*Gifts*—Three things happen at this point: (1) Guests and members are once again welcomed to the service and thanked for coming. They also receive an invitation to come again; (2) A few brief announcements are made; and (3) A short, nonthreatening introduction prepares people for the offering.

*Special Music*—A solo or small-group piece is performed during the taking of the offering, setting the focus for the message.

*The Message*

*Closing*—a time of prayer relating to the message. A period of silence may be observed (with background music), or the ensemble might sing an appropriate song, calling people to commitment, followed by silent prayer. After the prayer, people can be invited to the prayer room, if one is available.

*Before the benediction, remind the audience of next week's theme and encourage them to invite a friend. Taking a moment after the benediction to thank people for worshiping sends a final note of warmth.

## Format #2

In this service, the offering follows the message. Act 1 of the format includes: celebration, message preparation, and the message. Act 2 focuses on the response to the message. The offering bridges the gap between the two acts.

*Call To Worship*

*Welcome*

*\*Worship Chorus*

*The Bible Reading and Prayer*

*Special Feature*

*Special Music*

*The Message*—Soft music behind a closing prayer will help smooth the transition from the message to the offering.

*Gifts*

*Special Music*

*Closing*

## Formats #3 and #4

These two formats add a worship chorus before the welcome.

| | |
|---|---|
| *Call to Worship* | *Call to Worship* |
| *\*Worship Chorus* | *\*Worship Chorus* |

Choose a chorus that maintains the climate of energy set in the call to worship.

| | |
|---|---|
| *Welcome* | *Welcome* |
| *\*Worship Choruses* | *\*Worship Choruses* |

(one to two choruses in this section)

133

APPENDIX A

| | |
|---|---|
| *Bible Reading and Prayer* | *Bible Reading and Prayer* |
| *Special Feature* | *Special Feature* |
| *Special Music* | *Special Music* |
| *Gifts* | *The Message* |
| *Special Music* | *Gifts* |
| *Message* | *Special Music* |
| *Closing* | *Closing* |

### Formats #5 and #6

In these variations, the drama or interview comes directly before the message as a way of setting it up.

| | |
|---|---|
| *Call To Worship* | *Call to Worship* |
| *Welcome* | *Welcome* |
| *\*Chorus* | *\*Chorus* |
| *Bible Reading and Prayer* | *Bible Reading and Prayer* |
| *Special Music* | *Special Music* |
| *Gifts* | *Drama/Interview* |
| *Special Music* | *The Message* |
| *Drama/Interview* | *Gifts* |
| *Message* | *Special Music* |
| *Closing* | *Closing* |

### Formats #7 and #8

These are communion formats. Communion essentially replaces the Special Feature.

| | |
|---|---|
| *Call to Worship* | *Call to Worship* |
| *Welcome* | *Welcome* |
| *\*Worship Chorus* | *\*Worship Chorus* |
| *Bible Reading and Prayer* | *Bible Reading and Prayer* |
| *Special Music* | *Special Music* |
| *Gifts* | *Message* |
| *Special Music* | *Gifts* |
| *The Message* | *Special Music* |
| *Communion* | *Communion* |

An introduction to communion is followed by a time for silence and reflection. After the assurance of forgiveness, the Words of Institution are shared. The Lord's Prayer may be used at this time. Giving detailed instructions on how to receive the elements will put guests at ease (if they are invited to participate). Congregational singing of worship choruses during communion will create a sense of excitement and celebration.

| | |
|---|---|
| *Closing* | *Closing* |

## II. Participational Services

These formats can be either believer-oriented or believer-oriented/visitor-sensitive. The target audience will determine the difference. The believer-oriented service will use language and message styles geared to Christians. The believer-oriented/visitor-sensitive service will cater to believers while attempting to put guests at ease, or it will make the needs of seekers the priority in choosing music and shaping the message.

Saddleback Valley Community Church in Mission Viejo, California, offers highly participational worship during its visitor-friendly services. However, the worship leaders use that participation as a presentation. Talented singers lead the worship, and if guests do not feel like singing or do not know the songs, they can simply listen. The singing of worship choruses, led by the musicians, becomes almost a concert in itself. Rick Warren, senior pastor of Saddleback, suggests that the larger the church becomes, the more participatory music it can use. An unchurched person standing and singing among fifty people might feel self-conscious, but in a crowd of one thousand, he or she can listen without having to sing.

Dramas and interviews can be used in these formats. See the presentational formats for placement suggestions.

One note of caution: Watch the amount of standing. Standing too long or too often wears people out.

### Format #9

This service is a blend of traditional and contemporary elements. Blended services, if not done well, have the potential of alienating everyone. Those preferring a more traditional, classical service will be upset with the contemporary choruses and music. Those enjoying the more contemporary styles will be turned off by the classical expressions.

Generally, in this type of worship, a moderate approach proves most successful: Not too heavy on the classical and not too up-tempo with the contemporary. Many middle-of-the-road contemporary songs fit nicely in a traditional service. A wise music director will use sensitivity in implementing this format.

*Call to Worship*—choir or ensemble.
*Welcome*
*\*Hymns*—a couple of solid, singable hymns. (Do not feel bound to sing all ten verses of each hymn.)

# APPENDIX A

*Prayer of Confession*—a brief order for confession and forgiveness, or other liturgical confessions.

*\*Worship Choruses*—three to four choruses or hymns of varying tempo. A contemplative climate can be set by ending with a slower, more worshipful, song or hymn. Have the congregation stand for the final chorus or two.

**Bible Reading**
**The Apostles' Creed**
*Special Music*—solo or appropriate choral piece. This sets the stage for the message.

**The Message**
**Tithes and Offerings**
*Special Music*—during the taking of the offering.

**The Lord's Prayer**
**Benediction**

The communion variation: Shorten the worship segment. Move the Prayer of Confession to the Celebration of Communion which follows the offering.

## Formats #10 and #11:

Both of these are contemporary, participational formats.

| | |
|---|---|
| *Call to Worship* | *Call to Worship* |
| *Welcome* | *Welcome* |
| *\*Worship Choruses* | *\*Worship Choruses* |

Sing three to four upbeat choruses, depending on the length of the service.

| | |
|---|---|
| *Bible Reading and Prayer* | *Bible Reading and Prayer* |
| *\*Worship Choruses* | *\*Worship Choruses* |

Include three to four more choruses, some upbeat, some contemplative. Time also will dictate the length of this segment. Again, have the audience stand for the last chorus or two.

| | |
|---|---|
| *Gifts* | *The Message* |
| *Special Music* | *Gifts* |
| *The Message* | *Special Music* |
| *Closing* | *Closing* |

## Formats #12 and #13

These formats put one worship segment before the welcome.

| | |
|---|---|
| *Call to Worship* | *Call to Worship* |
| *\*Worship Choruses* | *\*Worship Choruses* |

Two up-tempo songs.

| | |
|---|---|
| *Welcome* | *Welcome* |
| *\*Worship Choruses* | *\*Worship Choruses* |

Three to four songs of varying tempo. Watch the standing!

| | |
|---|---|
| *Bible Reading and Prayer* | *Bible Reading and Prayer* |
| *Special Music* | *Special Music* |
| *Gifts* | *The Message* |
| *Special Music* | *Gifts* |
| *The Message* | *Special Music* |
| *Closing* | *Closing* |

**Formats #14 and #15**

| | |
|---|---|
| *Call to Worship* | *Call to Worship* |
| *Welcome* | *Welcome* |
| *\*Worship* | *\*Worship* |

This is an extended period of worship, lasting 15 to 25 minutes, and using varying tempos and styles.

| | |
|---|---|
| *Special Music* | *Special Music* |

This can be optional.

| | |
|---|---|
| *Gifts* | *The Message* |
| *Special Music* | *Gifts* |
| *The Message* | *Special Music* |
| *Closing* | *Closing* |

In formats 10, 12, and 14, communion follows the message. In formats 11, 13, and 15, communion follows the offering. Time restraints may mean shortening the opening worship segments.

Again, many of these participational formats can be used in believer-oriented services. The leadership, message content, and style will change, but the basic formats can remain the same.

## III. Reviewing the Service

Careful, honest evaluation of the service leads to more effective worship experiences. Videotaping the service will give the worship team a chance to evaluate themselves. Recruiting people to evaluate the service as it happens offers the "consumer's" view. Using evaluators from the target audience (i.e., former unchurched members) will provide invaluable insights. Keep in mind that God's Spirit works even when all does not go as we planned. His Word will not return void!

# SERVICE EVALUATION FORM
## (This form follows Format #1)

Service Date:_____    Service Time:_____

Key:  1 = Forgive and forget
      2 = Needs improvement
      3 = Good, but don't stop there
      4 = Keep it up!
      5 = Bull's-eye!

Try to evaluate the service from the perspective of a guest or one unfamiliar with the church or the gospel.

## PRELUDE

| | | | | | |
|---|---|---|---|---|---|
| Climate | 1 | 2 | 3 | 4 | 5 |
| Appropriateness | 1 | 2 | 3 | 4 | 5 |
| Volume | 1 | 2 | 3 | 4 | 5 |

Comments:  _____

_____


## CALL TO WORSHIP

| | | | | | |
|---|---|---|---|---|---|
| Climate | 1 | 2 | 3 | 4 | 5 |
| Enthusiasm | 1 | 2 | 3 | 4 | 5 |
| Appropriateness | 1 | 2 | 3 | 4 | 5 |
| Quality | 1 | 2 | 3 | 4 | 5 |
| Presentation | 1 | 2 | 3 | 4 | 5 |

Comments:  _____

_____


## WELCOME

| | | | | | |
|---|---|---|---|---|---|
| Climate | 1 | 2 | 3 | 4 | 5 |
| Enthusiasm | 1 | 2 | 3 | 4 | 5 |
| Delivery | 1 | 2 | 3 | 4 | 5 |

Comments:  _____

_____

## CHORUSES

| | | | | | |
|---|---|---|---|---|---|
| Singability | 1 | 2 | 3 | 4 | 5 |
| Leadership | 1 | 2 | 3 | 4 | 5 |
| Content | 1 | 2 | 3 | 4 | 5 |

Comments: _____

_____


## BIBLE READING AND PRAYER

| | | | | | |
|---|---|---|---|---|---|
| Delivery | 1 | 2 | 3 | 4 | 5 |
| Understandability | 1 | 2 | 3 | 4 | 5 |
| Length | 1 | 2 | 3 | 4 | 5 |

Comments: _____

_____


## SPECIAL FEATURE

| | | | | | |
|---|---|---|---|---|---|
| Message (content) | 1 | 2 | 3 | 4 | 5 |
| Length | 1 | 2 | 3 | 4 | 5 |
| Quality | 1 | 2 | 3 | 4 | 5 |

Comments: _____

_____


## SPECIAL MUSIC

| | | | | | |
|---|---|---|---|---|---|
| Quality | 1 | 2 | 3 | 4 | 5 |
| Presentation | 1 | 2 | 3 | 4 | 5 |
| Message | 1 | 2 | 3 | 4 | 5 |
| Relevance | 1 | 2 | 3 | 4 | 5 |
| Tempo | 1 | 2 | 3 | 4 | 5 |

Comments: _____

_____


## ANNOUNCEMENTS/GIFTS

| | | | | | |
|---|---|---|---|---|---|
| Delivery | 1 | 2 | 3 | 4 | 5 |
| Number | 1 | 2 | 3 | 4 | 5 |
| Relevance | 1 | 2 | 3 | 4 | 5 |
| Appeal | 1 | 2 | 3 | 4 | 5 |

Comments: _____

_____

## OFFERING MUSIC

| | | | | | |
|---|---|---|---|---|---|
| Quality | 1 | 2 | 3 | 4 | 5 |
| Presentation | 1 | 2 | 3 | 4 | 5 |
| Message | 1 | 2 | 3 | 4 | 5 |
| Relevance | 1 | 2 | 3 | 4 | 5 |
| Tempo | 1 | 2 | 3 | 4 | 5 |

Comments _____

_____


## THE MESSAGE

| | | | | | |
|---|---|---|---|---|---|
| Content | 1 | 2 | 3 | 4 | 5 |
| Relevance | 1 | 2 | 3 | 4 | 5 |
| Applicability | 1 | 2 | 3 | 4 | 5 |
| Length | 1 | 2 | 3 | 4 | 5 |
| Use of Stories | 1 | 2 | 3 | 4 | 5 |
| Clarity | 1 | 2 | 3 | 4 | 5 |
| Facial Expressions | 1 | 2 | 3 | 4 | 5 |
| Voice Projection | 1 | 2 | 3 | 4 | 5 |
| Speed | 1 | 2 | 3 | 4 | 5 |
| Gestures | 1 | 2 | 3 | 4 | 5 |
| Listenability | 1 | 2 | 3 | 4 | 5 |

Comments: _____

_____


## CLOSING

| | | | | | |
|---|---|---|---|---|---|
| Relevance | 1 | 2 | 3 | 4 | 5 |
| Climate set | 1 | 2 | 3 | 4 | 5 |

Comments: _____

_____


## TECHNICAL

| | | | | | |
|---|---|---|---|---|---|
| Sound | 1 | 2 | 3 | 4 | 5 |
| Lighting | 1 | 2 | 3 | 4 | 5 |
| Staging | 1 | 2 | 3 | 4 | 5 |

Comments: _____

_____

THEME
Consistency        1     2     3     4     5

OTHER
Dead Spots         1     2     3     4     5
Communion          1     2     3     4     5
Ushering           1     2     3     4     5

OVERALL RATING 1     2     3     4     5

BRAVO! _____

_____

NEEDS WORK:_____

_____

*If we don't keep up
with the future,
our customers
will pass us by.*

# APPENDIX B
## Resources

Contemporary music, by its nature, becomes dated quickly. A staff person or volunteer committed to staying musically current will help keep a congregation on the "cutting edge." The resources listed below will help congregations get started. Most of those listed here and many others can be found through local Christian bookstores.

### Copyright

Christian Copyright Licensing, Inc., 6130 NE 78th Ct., Suite C11, Portland OR 97218-2853, 1-800-234-2446.

This blanket license covers most major religious music publishers. It allows a congregation to print the words to songs in the worship bulletin. Call or write for fees and information.

### Hymnals/Songbooks/Worship Choruses

Check with your denominational publishing house. Many have produced their own contemporary worship resources.

*Hymns for the Family of God* (Nashville: Paragon Associates, Inc., 1976).
*Integrity* (new, up-to-date worship choruses offered on a periodic series basis) 1000 Cody Road, Mobile AL 36695, 1-800-239-7000.

*Maranatha! Music Praise Chorus Book* (Costa Mesa: Maranatha!, Distributed by Word Music, 1983).

*The Other Song Book* (Phoenix: The Fellowship Publications, 6202 South Maple, Suite 121, Tempe AZ 85283, 1987). 1-602-838-8500

*Spirit Touching Spirit* (Minneapolis: Prince of Peace Publishing, 13801 Fairview Drive, Burnsville MN 55337, 1987). 1-612-435-8102

## Choral/Ensemble/Solo Music

Choral and ensemble music can be found through most local Christian bookstores or through publishing houses. The director of music can also network with others to find other sources for music.

Brentwood Music, 316 South Gate Court, Brentwood TN 37027, 1-800-846-7664.

Hope Publishing, 380 S. Main Place, Carol Stream IL 60188, 1-800-323-1049.

Lillenas Publishing Co. (Beacon Hill Press), P.O. Box 419527, Kansas City MO 64141, 1-800-877-0700.

The Lorenz Corp., 501 East 3rd Street, P.O. Box 802, Dayton OH 45401, 1-800-444-1144.

Sparrow Corp., 101 Winners Circle, Brentwood TN 37027, 1-800-877-4443.

Word Music, Inc., P.O. Box 2518, Waco TX 76702, 1-800-933-9673.

Zondervan Corp./Benson Music Group 5300 Patterson Ave S.E., Grand Rapids MI 49530, 1-800-727-1390.

Local Christian bookstores should also have many background tapes available for soloists and ensembles.

## Drama

Most Christian dramas focus on believers. Very few seek to speak to and reach irreligious people. Congregations may have to recruit their own writers. Many churches may be surprised by the writing talent in their congregations and community.

Community Church of Joy provides sketches for a small fee. Joy Resources, P.O. Box 6030, Glendale AZ 85312, 1-602-938-1460.

The Jeremiah People and dramas published by Lillenas (Beacon Hill Press) offer a good starting point. They can be found in most Christian bookstores.

# RESOURCES

Willow Creek Community Church provides perhaps the best resource for visitor-oriented dramas. Their scripts can be purchased for a small fee from Willow Creek Resources, Zondervan Direct Source, 5300 Patterson SE, Grand Rapids MI 49530, 1-800-876-SEEK (7335), 1-708-765-6208.

## Magazines

*Contemporary Christian Music Magazine* serves as a great resource for music ministers. It focuses on the latest trends and styles in Contemporary Christian Music. CCM, P.O. Box 55995, Boulder CO 80322, 1-800-333-9643.

## Preaching Resources

*Illustration Digest*, P.O. Box 170, Winslow AZ 72959. Published six times per year for a yearly fee. Filled with illustrations.

*Leadership Magazine*, 465 Gundersen Drive, Carol Stream, IL 60188. In addition to being an excellent magazine, *Leadership* offers a two-page section called "To Illustrate . . ."

*The Pastor's Story File* and *Parables, etc.*, P.O. Box 8, Plateville CO 80651-0008. *The Pastor's Story File*, published monthly, offers stories and illustrations based on a certain theme. *Parables, etc.*, also published monthly, features a host of stories on varying topics. Both are available through subscription.

*Plus Magazine*, Foundation for Christian Living, P.O. Box FCL, Pawling NY 12564. Mailed each month, *Plus Magazine* offers three articles, most of them written by Dr. Norman Vincent Peale. Each article utilizes plenty of stories. A small yearly donation is requested.

*Robert Schuller Ministries*, Box 100, Garden Grove CA 92642. Dr. Schuller always fills his messages with great stories. For a small yearly fee pastors receive four sermons each month.

Newspapers, magazine articles, sociological studies, and other resources provide excellent stats and stories. If retelling the story of a member, be sure to get permission first.

## Sermon Series/Titles Examples

**Series Title:** Getting to Know the God Who Loves You
How to Know God Personally (John 17:3; John 1:12)

147

How to Make Sense Out of the Bible (Psalm 119:105)
How to Talk with God (Revelation 3:20)
Inviting Others to Know the God Who Loves Them (Acts 1:8)

**Series Title:** The Gift of Human Sexuality
The Uniqueness of a Man (Psalm 8:3-8)
The Uniqueness of a Woman (Genesis 2:18-22)
Keys to Healthy Male-Female Relationships (Genesis 1:27-28; Galatians 3:26-29)
Guilt-Free Sex (I Thessalonians 4:1-7)

**Series Title:** Healing the Hurts of the Past
Overcoming Shame (John 8:1-11)
Healing from Abuse (Matthew 12:15-21)
Dealing with Hurt and Anger (Ephesians 4:21)

**Series Title:** In Search of Fulfillment
In Search of Fulfillment (Isaiah 55:1-2; 6)
In Search of Fulfillment in Failed Expectations (Philippians 4:12-13)
In Search of Fulfillment in Relationships (Philippians 2:1-11)
In Search of Fulfillment Through Truth (John 8:31)
In Search of Fulfillment Through Commitment (Psalm 37:3-6)

**Series Title:** Making Your House a Home
Making Your House a Home (Matthew 7:24-27)
How to Affair-Proof Your Marriage (Ephesians 5:21-33)
Surviving Infidelity (Proverbs 6:27-39)
Dealing with Divorce (Matthew 19:3-9)
How to Enjoy the Single Life (John 10:10)
How to Raise Positive Children (Ephesians 6:4)

**Series Title:** Taking the Chaos Out of Life
Time Management (Psalm 118:24-25)
Stress Management (Isaiah 26:3-4)
Financial Management (Matthew 6:33)

## Recommended Reading

George Barna, *The Invisible Generation: Baby Busters* (Barna Research Group, 647 W. Broadway, Glendale CA 91204, 1992).
William Dunn, *The Baby Bust: A Generation Comes of Age* (Ithaca, N.Y.: American Demographics Books, 1993).
George G. Hunter III, *How to Reach Secular People* (Nashville: Abingdon Press, 1992).

# RESOURCES

Bill Hybels, Stuart Briscoe and Haddon Robinson, *Mastering Contemporary Preaching* (Portland: Multnomah, 1989).

Loren Mead, *The Once and Future Church* (The Alban Institute, 4125 Nebraska Ave. N.W., Washington DC 20016, 1991).

Herb Miller, *The Vital Congregation* (Nashville: Abingdon Press, 1990).

Doug Murren, *The Baby Boomerang: Catching Baby Boomers As They Return to Church* (Ventura: Regal Books, 1990).

Wade Clark Roof, *A Generation of Seekers: The Spiritual Journeys of the Baby Boom Generation* (San Francisco: HarperCollins, 1993).

Lyle Schaller, *It's a Different World* (Nashville: Abingdon Press, 1987).

Norman Shawchuck et al., *Marketing for Congregations* (Nashville: Abingdon Press, 1992).

## Institutes and Seminars

Community Church of Joy Academy for Evangelism and Church Growth, P.O. Box 6030, Glendale AZ 85312

The Robert H. Schuller Institute for Successful Church Leadership, 1241 Lewis Street, Garden Grove CA 92640

Saddleback Valley Community Church, 23456 Madero, Suite 100, Mission Viejo CA 92691

Willow Creek Community Church, 67 E. Algonquin Road, Barrington IL 60010

# NOTES

### I. "We've Never Done It That Way Before!"

1. Eric Miller, *Future Vision* (Naperville, Ill.: Sourcebooks Trade, 1991), p. 143.

### II. Liturgical Worship and the Unchurched

1. Bob Orr, "Worship that Attracts and Holds the Unchurched," seminar at Community Church of Joy, Phoenix, Arizona (February 4, 1991).

2. Ibid.

### IV. Contemporary Worship: Laying the Foundation

1. Bob Orr, "Worship that Attracts and Holds the Unchurched," seminar at Community Church of Joy, Phoenix, Arizona (February 4, 1991).

### V. Designing a Contemporary Outreach-oriented Service

1. George Barna, *Ministry Currents* (January-March 1992), p. 11.

### VI. Preaching and the Unchurched

1. Rick Warren, "How to Plant a Church," conference sponsored by Charles E. Fuller Institute of Evangelism and Church Growth (November 18-20, 1986).

2. Dieter Zander, "Baby Busters: How to Reach a New Generation," *The Pastor's Update* (a monthly tape series), Charles E. Fuller Institute of Evangelism and Church Growth (November 1992).

3. Lewis B. Smedes, *How Can It Be All Right When Everything Is All Wrong?* (New York: Harper & Row, 1982), pp. 80-81.

## VII. Preaching to Irreligious People

1. Barbara Robinson, *The Best Christmas Pageant Ever* (New York: Avon Books, 1972), p. 1.

2. Ibid, pp. 39-40, 43-45, 47-48.

3. George Barna, *What Americans Believe: An Annual Survey of Values and Views in the United States* (Ventura, Calif.: Regal Books, 1991), pp. 152-58.

4. George Barna, *Ministry Currents* (January-March 1992), pp. 11-12.

5. Stuart Brisco, "Pulpits of Wood to Pulpits That Would," *Church Disciple* (November 1992), pp. 2-3.

6. R.C.H. Lenski, *Commentary on Ephesians* (Columbus, Ohio: Wartburg Press, 1946), p. 593.

7. George G. Hunter III, *How to Reach Secular People* (Nashville: Abingdon Press, 1992), p. 92; quoting Alan Walker, *The Whole Gospel for the Whole World* (Nashville: Abingdon Press, 1959), p. 59.

8. Ibid.

## VIII. Fine-tuning

1. From Steven Curtis Chapman and Geoff Moore, *The Great Adventure*, Sparrow Song (a division of the Sparrow Corp.) and Careers-BMG Music Publishing, Inc./Peach Hill Songs/Starstruck Music (a division of Forefront Communications Group, Inc.), 1992.